"Equal parts family saga, grief narrative, a̶n̶..."
—*THE NEW YORK TIMES*

"An unflinchingly honest look inside the First Family."
—*ENTERTAINMENT WEEKLY*

"In an era of indulgent political memoirs that seek to promote
a candidate's platform and cast the family as picture-perfect,
Beautiful Things stands out for its raw truths."
—*TIME.COM*

"I've never read a memoir like this before . . .
It is extraordinary . . . It's breathtaking."
—BRIAN STELTER, CNN's *Reliable Sources*

"As honest an account of addiction and grief as is possible . . .
one we can all, in some way, see ourselves or our families
or our hearts in at the same time."
—*VANITY FAIR*

"So concise, so unflinching and propulsive, that outside of
turning the pages and occasionally picking my jaw off the ground,
I didn't move between the first page and the last."
—DAVE EGGERS, *New York Times* bestselling author

"Hunter Biden writes beautifully of almost unsurvivable loss, and the
amazing grace of family love . . . He writes of his savage alcoholism
and addiction with rare honesty, of his recovery with stunned
gratitude, of broken hearts, resurrection, beautiful things."
—ANNE LAMOTT, *New York Times* bestselling author

"Hunter's unflinching account lays bare both the sustaining
power and hard limits of love and family."
—BILL CLEGG, *New York Times* bestselling author

BEAUTIFUL
THINGS

BEAUTIFUL THINGS

A MEMOIR

HUNTER BIDEN

GALLERY BOOKS

NEW YORK LONDON TORONTO SYDNEY NEW DELHI

G

Gallery Books
An Imprint of Simon & Schuster, Inc.
1230 Avenue of the Americas
New York, NY 10020

First Gallery Books trade paperback edition May 2022

GALLERY BOOKS and colophon are registered trademarks of Simon & Schuster, Inc.

For information about special discounts for bulk purchases, please contact Simon & Schuster Special Sales at 1-866-506-1949 or business@simonandschuster.com.

The Simon & Schuster Speakers Bureau can bring authors to your live event. For more information or to book an event, contact the Simon & Schuster Speakers Bureau at 1-866-248-3049 or visit our website at www.simonspeakers.com.

Interior design by Jaime Putorti

Manufactured in the United States of America

10 9 8 7 6 5 4 3 2 1

Library of Congress Control Number: 2021932577

ISBN 978-1-9821-5111-9
ISBN 978-1-9821-5112-6 (pbk)
ISBN 978-1-9821-5113-3 (ebook)

For my family

the curious feeling

swam through him

that everything

was

beautiful

there,

that it would always

stay beautiful

there.

—FROM "NIRVANA,"

BY CHARLES BUKOWSKI

CONTENTS

Prologue: "Where's Hunter?"   1

Chapter One: Seventeen Minutes   9

Chapter Two: Requiem   29

Chapter Three: Growing Up Biden   45

Chapter Four: Loaded   66

Chapter Five: Falling   95

Chapter Six: Burisma   117

Chapter Seven: Cracked   135

Chapter Eight: Into the Desert   151

Chapter Nine: California Odyssey   183

Chapter Ten: Lost Highway   199

Chapter Eleven: Saved   212

Epilogue: Dear Beau   239

Afterword   249

Acknowledgments   259

PROLOGUE

"WHERE'S HUNTER?"

As I began writing this book from the relative calm of my home office, in November 2019, I sat in the center of a political firestorm, the consequences of which could change the course of history.

The president of the United States was smearing me almost daily from the South Lawn of the White House. He invoked my name at rallies to incite his base. "Where's Hunter?" replaced "Lock her up!" as his go-to hype line. If you wanted, you could even buy a WHERE'S HUNTER? T-shirt directly from his campaign website—twenty-five dollars, sizes small to 3XL.

Not long after that call to arms became part of his stock repertoire, supporters sporting blood-red MAGA caps appeared outside the driveway gate of the private house I was renting in Los Angeles with my wife, Melissa, then five months pregnant. They snarled through bullhorns and waved posters depicting me as the titular character from *Where's Waldo?* Red hats and photographers followed

1

us in cars. We called the police, as did some of our neighbors, to shoo them away. Yet threats—including an anonymous text to one of my daughters at school, warning her that they knew where I lived—forced us to seek a safer address. Melissa was scared to death—for her, for us, for our baby.

I became a proxy for Donald Trump's fear that he wouldn't be reelected. He pushed debunked conspiracy theories about work I did in Ukraine and China, even as his own children had pocketed millions in China and Russia and his former campaign manager sat in a jail cell for laundering millions more from Ukraine. He did all this while his shadow foreign policy, led by his personal attorney Rudy Giuliani, unraveled in plain sight.

It was a predictable enough tactic, straight from the playbook of his dark-arts mentor, Roy Cohn, the grand wizard of McCarthyism. I expected the president to get far more personal far earlier to exploit the demons and addictions I've dealt with for years. Early on, at least, he ceded that tactic to his trolls. One morning as I was working on the book, I looked up at a TV screen to see Matt Gaetz, a Florida congressman and Trump henchman, read a magazine excerpt that detailed my addiction straight into the record of the House Judiciary Committee's hearing on articles of impeachment.

"I don't want to make light of anybody's substance abuse issues . . ." Gaetz said, snickering for the cameras as he made light of my substance abuse issues.

"Again, I'm not . . . casting any judgment on any challenges someone goes through in their personal life," Gaetz continued, as he cast judgment on my personal life.

This from someone once arrested for driving under the influence in his daddy's BMW, and who later had the charges mysteriously dropped. Anything to keep the reality-TV narrative running.

None of that matters in an up-is-down, Orwellian political climate. Trump believed that if he could destroy me, and by extension my father, he could dispatch any candidate of decency from either party—all while diverting attention from his own corrupt behavior.

Where's Hunter?

I'm right here. I've faced and survived worse. I've known the extremes of success and ruin. With my mother and baby sister killed in a car accident when I was two, my father suffering a life-threatening brain aneurysm and embolism in his forties, and my brother dying way too young from a horrible brain cancer, I come from a family forged by tragedies and bound by a remarkable, unbreakable love.

I'm not going anywhere. I'm not a curio or sideshow to a moment in history, as all the cartoonish attacks try to paint me. I'm not Billy Carter or Roger Clinton, God bless them. I am not Eric Trump or Donald Trump Jr.—I've worked for someone other than my father, rose and fell on my own. This book will establish that.

For the record:

I'm a fifty-one-year-old father who helped raise three beautiful daughters, two in college and one who graduated last year from law school, and now a year-old son. I earned degrees from Yale Law and Georgetown, where I've also taught in the master's program of the School of Foreign Service.

I've been a senior executive at one of the country's largest financial institutions (since acquired by Bank of America), founded my own multinational firms, and worked as counsel for Boies Schiller Flexner, which represents many of the largest and most sophisticated organizations in the world.

I've served on the board of directors at Amtrak (appointed by Republican president George W. Bush) and chaired the board of the nonprofit World Food Program USA, part of the largest hunger-relief mission on the planet. As part of my voluntary position for the WFP, I traveled to refugee camps and areas devastated by natural disasters around the globe—Syria, Kenya, the Philippines. I've sat with traumatized families inside homes fashioned out of aluminum shipping containers, then briefed members of Congress, or talked directly with heads of state, about how best to provide swift, life-saving relief.

Before that, I lobbied for Jesuit universities. I helped secure funding for mobile dental clinics in underserved Detroit, after-school training programs for teachers in lower-income neighborhoods in Philadelphia, and a mental health facility for underprivileged and disabled veterans in Cincinnati.

My point: I've done serious work for serious people. There's no question that my last name has opened doors, but my qualifications and accomplishments speak for themselves. That those accomplishments sometimes crossed my father's spheres of influence during his two terms as vice president—how could they not? What I did misjudge, however, was the notion that Trump would become president and, once in office, act with impunity and vengeance for his political gain.

That's on me. That's on all of us.

Then there is this:

I'm also an alcoholic and a drug addict. I've bought crack cocaine on the streets of Washington, DC, and cooked up my own inside a hotel bungalow in Los Angeles. I've been so desperate for a drink that I couldn't make the one-block walk between a liquor store and my apartment without uncapping the bottle to take a swig. In the last five years alone, my two-decades-long marriage has dissolved, guns have been put in my face, and at one point I dropped clean off the grid, living in $59-a-night Super 8 motels off I-95 while scaring my family even more than myself.

That deep descent came not long after I hugged my brother, Beau, the best friend I've ever had and the person I loved most in the world, as he took his last breath. Beau and I talked virtually every day of our lives. While we argued as adults almost as much as we laughed, we never ended a conversation without one of us saying, "I love you," and the other responding, "I love you, too."

After Beau died, I never felt more alone. I lost hope.

I've since pulled out of that dark, bleak hole. It's an outcome that was unthinkable in early 2019. My recovery never could have happened without the unconditional love of my father and the everlasting love of my brother, which has carried on after his death.

The love between me and my father and Beau—the most profound love I've ever known—is at the heart of this memoir. It's a love that allowed me to continue these last five years in the midst of both personal demons and pressure from the outside world writ large, including a president's unhinged fury.

It's a Biden love story, of course, which means it's complicated: tragic, humane, emotional, enduring, widely consequential, and ultimately redemptive. It carries on no matter what. My dad has often said that Beau was his soul and I am his heart. That about nails it.

I thought of those words often as they related to my life. Beau was my soul, too. I've learned that it's conceivable to go on living without a soul as long as your heart is still beating. But figuring out how to live when your soul has been ripped from you—when it has been so thoroughly extinguished that you find yourself buying crack in the middle of the night behind a gas station in Nashville, Tennessee, or craving the tiny liquor bottles in your hotel minibar while sitting in a palace in Amman with the king of Jordan—well, that's a more problematic process.

There are millions of others still living in the dark place where I was, or far worse. Their circumstances might be different, their resources far fewer, but the pain, shame, and hopelessness of addiction are the same for everyone. I lived in those crack motels. I spent time with "those" people—rode with them, scoured the streets with them, got high as a fucking kite with them. It left me with an overwhelming empathy for those struggling just to make it from one moment to the next.

Yet even in the depths of my addiction, when I washed up in the most wretched places, I found extraordinary things. Generosities were extended to me by people society considers untouchables. I finally understood how we are all connected by a common humanity, if not also by a common Maker.

Mine is an unlikely résumé for this sort of confession. Believe me, I get it. Yet as desperate, dangerous, and lunatic as that résumé often is, it also teems with basic, affirming connections.

I want those still living in the black hole of alcoholism and drug abuse to see themselves in my plight and then to take hope in my escape, at least so far. We're all alone in our addiction. It doesn't matter how much money you have, who your friends are, the family you come from. In the end, we all have to deal with it ourselves— first one day, then another one, and then the next.

And I want to illuminate, with honesty and humility and not just a little awe, how family love was my only effective defense against the many demons I ran up against.

Writing this book wasn't easy. Sometimes it was cathartic; other times it was triggering. I've pushed away from my desk more than once while putting down thoughts about my last four years wandering the wilderness of alcoholism and crack addiction—memories too breathtaking, too disturbing, or still too close not to give me pause. There were times when I literally trembled, felt my stomach clench and my forehead perspire in too-familiar ways.

When I was not quite a year sober, as I worked on the early parts of this book, crack remained the first thing I thought about every morning when I woke up. I became like some feverish war reenactor, meticulously going through the rituals of my addiction, pathetic step by pathetic step—minus the drug, and with Melissa asleep beside me. I reached an arm over to the side table next to the bed and fumbled around for a piece of crack. I imagined finding one, then imagined inserting it into a pipe, drawing it to my lips, igniting it with a lighter, and then experiencing the sensation of complete and utter well-being. It was the most alluring, most enticing . . .

Then I'd catch myself and stop. Melissa would awaken and a new day, free from all that, would begin. My dad would call from a primary stop in Iowa or Texas or Pennsylvania. My oldest daughter would call from law school in New York, asking me again if I'd read the paper she'd sent for me to look over. A hawk would whirl above the canyon outside my window, teasingly, tauntingly, beautifully, and all I could think of was Beau. Yet as far as I'd come, those old, bad days never felt far away.

This is the story of my journey, from there to here.

CHAPTER ONE

SEVENTEEN MINUTES

We took Beau off life support late on the morning of May 29, 2015. He was unresponsive and barely breathing. Doctors in the critical care unit of the Walter Reed National Military Medical Center, in Bethesda, Maryland, told us he would pass within hours of their removing his tracheostomy tube. I knew he would hold on longer—that was Beau. So I sat at my big brother's bedside and held his hand.

A throng of family stood by as well—twenty-four Bidens slipping in and out of the room, wandering the hospital's halls, lost in thought, waiting. I didn't leave Beau's side.

The morning seeped into the afternoon, then into the evening, then late into the night. The sun came back up, its light scarcely leaking through the room's drawn shades. It was a confusing, excruciating time: I wished for a miracle and for an end to my brother's suffering, both in the same prayer.

More hours crawled past. I talked to Beau continuously. I whispered in his ear how much I loved him. I told him that I knew how much he loved me. I told him we would always be together, that nothing could ever separate us. I told him how proud of him I was, how fiercely he had fought to hold on, through surgeries and radiation and a final experimental procedure, in which an engineered virus was injected directly into his tumor—directly into his brain.

He never stood a chance.

He was forty-six.

Yet from the moment of his diagnosis less than two years earlier, and throughout those many procedures, Beau's mantra to me became two words: "Beautiful things." He insisted that when he got well, we would dedicate our lives to appreciating and cultivating the world's boundless beauty. "Beautiful things" became a catchall for relationships and places and moments—for everything. Once this was over, he said, we would start a law firm together and work on only "beautiful things." We would rock on the porch of our parents' house and look out at the "beautiful things" spread before us. We would luxuriate in the "beautiful things" our children and families became during each incremental passage along the way.

It was our code for a renewed outlook on life. We would never again let ourselves get too tired, too distracted, too cynical, too thrown off course by whatever blindsiding hurdle life threw in our way, to *look*, to *see*, to *love*.

*   *   *

"I love you. I love you. I love you."

I've had a single flash of memory from the earliest and most consequential moment of my life. I can't be sure how much of it is a composite of family stories and news accounts I've heard or read through the years, and how much of it is actual repressed memory finally trickling up to the fore.

But it's vivid.

It is December 18, 1972. My dad has just won the race for junior U.S. senator from Delaware—he turned thirty three weeks after the election, barely beating the Senate's age requirement before taking his oath in January. He is in Washington, DC, that day to interview staff for his new office. My mother, Neilia, beautiful and brilliant and also only thirty, has taken me; my big brother, Beau; and our baby sister, Naomi, Christmas-tree shopping near our fixer-upper house in Wilmington.

Beau is almost four. I'm almost three. We were born a year and a day apart—virtually Irish twins.

In my mind's eye, this is what happens next:

I'm seated in the back of our roomy white Chevy station wagon, behind my mother. Beau is back there with me, behind Naomi, whom we both call Caspy—pale, plump, and seeming to have appeared in our family out of nowhere thirteen months earlier, she was nicknamed after one of our favorite cartoon characters, Casper the Friendly Ghost. She's sound asleep in the front passenger seat, tucked into a bassinet.

Suddenly, I see my mother's head turn to the right. I don't remember anything else about her profile: the look in her eye, the expression of her mouth. Her head simply swings. At that same moment, my brother dives—or is hurtled—straight toward me.

That's it. It's quick and convulsive and chaotic: as our mother eased the car into a four-way intersection, we were broadsided by a tractor trailer carrying corncobs.

My mother and little sister were killed almost instantly. Beau was pulled from the wreckage with a broken leg and myriad other injuries. I suffered a severe skull fracture.

The next thing I remember is waking up in a hospital with Beau in the bed next to mine, bandaged and in traction, looking like he's just been clobbered in a playground brawl. He's mouthing three words to me, over and over:

"I love you. I love you. I love you."

That's our origin story. Beau became my best friend, my soul mate, and my polestar since those virtually first conscious moments of my life.

Three weeks later, inside our hospital room, Dad was sworn into the Senate.

Beau was Delaware's two-term attorney general and father of a young daughter and son when doctors diagnosed him with glioblastoma multiforme—brain cancer.

It likely had incubated inside him for at least the previous three years. In the fall of 2010, about a year after he returned from deployment in Iraq, Beau complained of headaches, numbness, and paralysis. At the time, doctors attributed his symptoms to a stroke.

We monitored Beau's progress after that. Something seemed off. Beau would joke to friends that all of a sudden he heard music. It wasn't a joke to me: it was eerie. He couldn't figure it out, but looking back I'm sure it was the tumor impinging on a part of his brain that caused auditory hallucinations—a growth touching a neuron that triggered another neuron, and suddenly you're hearing Johnny Cash playing in the background. That's what Beau was experiencing.

Finally, on a warm early evening in August 2013, inside a small-town hospital in Michigan City, Indiana, I watched in horror as Beau endured a grand mal seizure. It confirmed that more sinister forces were at work. The day before, Beau had made the annual eleven-hour car trek from Delaware with his wife and kids to vacation with me and my family on Lake Michigan, not far from where my then-wife, Kathleen, grew up. I'd arrived at the summer house that day after spending the weekend serving in the U.S. Navy Reserve in Norfolk, Virginia, and was changing clothes to meet the whole crew at Kathleen's cousin's house, a block away, when I spotted Beau and our families walking back up the driveway. Everyone around him was in a panic.

Beau insisted he was fine. But he was clearly struggling, hunched over and unstable. We drove him to the local hospital, where technicians were about to perform an MRI when he had his seizure. It was terrifying, like something out of *The Exorcist*. The violence erupting inside his body was being expressed in convulsions and contractions; you could almost literally see the storm raging inside his brain. It seemed to last forever. I felt helpless: I wanted to absorb my brother's pain, yet there was nothing I could do.

Nothing.

When the storm finally passed, Beau was rushed by air ambulance to Northwestern Memorial Hospital in Chicago. His wife, Hallie, and I followed in my car, racing the whole way, making the seventy-minute drive in half the usual time. Beau had undergone an MRI by the time we arrived. The doctor showed us the images.

I was relieved. I'd looked at so many brain images since Beau's stroke that I thought I knew exactly what was going on.

"That's just the infarct," I said, referring to the part of the brain damaged by the stroke. It showed up as a dingy shadow.

The surgeon, one of the best in the country, let out a sympathetic sigh.

"Hunter," he said solemnly, "I think it's a tumor."

"No way," I insisted. "It's exactly . . . I've been looking at these images for over a year now. That's where the stroke occurred—exactly where it occurred."

"Well, I don't know about that," the surgeon said. "But this looks like a tumor."

We flew Beau home and took him to Thomas Jefferson University Hospital, close by in Philadelphia. The tumor was confirmed.

A few days later, Beau and I boarded a plane for Houston to meet with a brain surgeon at the University of Texas MD Anderson Cancer Center.

Glioblastoma multiforme is a mean, relentless horror. Doctors told Beau after his first surgery that it had been successful, that they'd removed all of the tumor they could see, but that it was the most aggressive type of cancer—a worst-case scenario. Nobody gave Beau the numbers—the odds—but I asked about them later when it was just Dad, me, and the surgeon in a room. I then looked it up online to make sure the survival rate he gave us was correct: less than one percent. Patients generally live from fourteen to eighteen months after diagnosis, and few who last longer than five years live with what's considered a bearable quality of life.

It was a death sentence.

I went quickly from disbelief to anger, sure that doctors had missed the tumor back when they'd determined he'd suffered a stroke. Would it have changed outcomes if they'd found it earlier? That's a different, unanswerable question.

Now Beau and the rest of us found ourselves in the same irre-solvable position many patients and families find themselves in after such a long-odds prognosis. We doubled down on what was almost surely a losing hand. Incapable, or unwilling, or just too damn scared to do otherwise, we adopted a fighting optimism about whatever procedures Beau's doctors recommended. Over the next twenty-one months, those recommendations included two more major brain surgeries, chemotherapy, and brutal radiation treatments—all, in the end, to no avail.

If I had to do it over, I never would have agreed to put Beau through the standard protocol, especially the radiation. Given the infinitesimal chances of his coming through it anything like he was before, and the pain and deficits it inflicted—difficulty talking, inabil-ity to put on shoes—it was almost barbaric. Yet in that moment, when you're in the hands of such brilliant, dedicated, and empathic professionals, even the slimmest chance seems worth pursuing.

Our final recourse was a high-risk, uncertain-reward option: the injection into his brain of a biological agent being developed by a research oncologist with funding from MD Anderson. We knew the chances of it reversing his cancer's advance were less than de minimis, yet we hoped for a miracle.

Hoping for a miracle is an oxymoron. By definition, a miracle is something a rational person can't rely on. So it takes a kind of dogged compartmentalizing to divorce yourself from rational thought at a time when you're immersed in nothing but calculated and rational decisions. In Beau's case, that meant everything from scheduling his procession of doctor's appointments to monitoring his diet to determining who was going to help him get dressed. Those banalities soon piled up into a kind of makeshift altar to the mystical, the magical, the unaccountable. We knew this procedure was a last resort—a true Hail Mary.

The time leading up to that final desperate measure, and the relatively short period that followed, also would be the last sublime stretch I spent with my brother.

Beau and I flew to Houston together the week before that last surgery at MD Anderson. We stayed in a hotel suite about a mile from the hospital, trekking there each day for the battery of tests and medicines needed to prep him for the procedure. Mom and Dad would arrive the day of the operation.

Beau had lost function to the degree that I had to put his socks and shoes on him, help him with the toilet, aid him in and out of the shower. We got in an argument shortly after we'd landed in Houston when I tried to set up an app on his phone to help him regulate his breathing, which had turned fickle. Beau got frustrated with himself when he couldn't do it the right way, then thought I was getting frustrated with him. It broke my heart that I needed to convince him otherwise: watching my older brother unable to follow instructions for something as basic as breathing in and out left me devastatingly sad.

Our time together that week alternated between a kind of biding quietude and laughing at the dumbest damn things. We didn't engage in heavy, this-could-be-it conversations; we never handicapped the procedure. We didn't make what-if preparations. We both knew intuitively what had to be done. Beau simply would not allow himself to plan for the worst. The rest of us took our cues from him.

Dad, as always, called constantly, asking if everything was all right and if there was anything he could do. My answers were almost always the same: yes, and no. He read into those responses what he needed to: in choppy times like these, he, Beau, and I could communicate through a kind of nonverbal frequency we'd developed during previous setbacks and tragedies. Saying much more risked breaking the spell and going to a place none of us wanted to go.

It wasn't as if we hadn't weighed more realistic thoughts. They just didn't need to be articulated right now. It wasn't like I didn't know what Beau wanted for me, or that I didn't know what I needed to do. It wasn't as if he had answers that I was failing to grasp, or vice versa.

One topic we did discuss aloud was how to handle his running for governor of Delaware after his surgery. Politics are in the Biden bloodstream. The current Democratic governor was term-limited, and Beau had announced the year before that he wouldn't seek reelection as attorney general so that he could focus on the 2016 governor's race. The unusual move to leave public service while seeking another position two years later fueled speculation about his health. We all knew the statistical probabilities of his diagnosis, but Beau approached it as if the treatments were going to work, and so we all acted likewise—damn the odds.

We remained more than hopeful about everything all week. That mindset was something beyond superstition for Beau. He made his way to the hospital each day like a pilgrim visiting some sacred site, convinced only good would come of it—that he could be cured. The doctors and staff, most of whom we knew well from his previous two surgeries there, became almost saintlike figures capable of transcendent things.

I recall especially Beau's fascination with the anesthesiologist, a great guy who had the most piercing blue eyes—eyes the very same blue, in fact, as my brother's. He intrigued Beau, and Beau talked all the time about the calming effect those eyes had on him. They were the last things Beau saw before the commencement of his two earlier craniotomies, and the first things Beau woke or became alert to afterward. The same anesthesiologist also sedated Beau before MRIs because of his fear of tight spaces. The two of them seemed to share some unspoken understanding as they stared into each other's identical deep-blue pools.

Back at the hotel, we laughed at the same things we'd always laughed at. I lay in bed with Beau while we streamed movies and TV shows on my laptop, staying there beside him until he drifted off to sleep. We binged *Curb Your Enthusiasm* and *Eastbound & Down*, both favorites of Beau's that traded on the sort of demented humor he ate up. But even then, he laughed a little less than he used to, seemed a little less amused. It became harder for him to follow storylines and maintain a sustained interest.

We didn't leave the room much—sometimes we ate downstairs at the hotel restaurant, one night we went out to see a movie, and another day two friends of Beau's surprised him by flying in for a visit. One afternoon we ventured into a nearby western-wear store. It was heartening to see some of Beau's humor peek through. He picked out a matching set of ridiculously bright red western shirts— they had buttons that snapped, making them easier for him to put on by himself—and he paired them with new blue jeans. I tried to convince him to get a cowboy hat, too, but he wouldn't bite. He wasn't that far gone. I bought it instead.

I cherished the hell out of that week. Looking back on it now, I see much of it as a ritual we both performed to prepare us for what was to come.

At first, everything seemed to go well. We hadn't gotten any post-op word yet from the doctor who performed the surgery, but Beau was conversational and in good spirits in the recovery room. Mom, Dad, and I hung around with him, sealed up in medical scrubs. I stayed behind after our parents left to go to a nearby conference room, their Secret Service detail posted throughout the building.

Having sat in too many hospital rooms with Beau during the past year, I noticed something flashing on a monitor that I knew wasn't good. I don't remember the metric it measured, but I do remember it was way too high. The surgeon spotted it the moment he walked in. His face flushed with alarm and he motioned for me to leave the room with him.

In the hallway, he said he was concerned. The surgery was technically exacting, essentially requiring him to thread a needle from the base of the skull and through the brain to deliver the agent into the tumor. Any variance as it passed through tissue could damage a critical component of the brain. He worried, as he put it to me then, "that I might have clipped something I shouldn't have." He wanted to review the data with his peers and raced off.

As we waited for him to return, Beau kept asking if something was wrong. I told him it was nothing, that the doc would be back any minute.

Five minutes passed. Then ten minutes. Then half an hour—at least that's how long the wait seemed to drag on for the two of us inside that white sanitized room. I didn't want to leave Beau, but I finally stepped outside and called Dad. In a panic, I told him I thought something had gone drastically wrong, that the doctor had disappeared and that couldn't be good. Dad chuckled: the doctor was standing beside him. The vice presidential protocol—alerting my dad before anyone else on matters that involved him directly—was followed in such situations and sometimes, like now, it left me in the lurch. The doctor had just given my parents a briefing and said that everything was fine.

It didn't stay fine for long.

Flown back to Delaware a few days later, Beau had one good night at his house with Hallie and their kids. The next day Hallie called me frantically in Washington to say Beau was unresponsive. I drove to Wilmington and went straight upstairs to his bedroom, where he hadn't reacted to anyone all day.

Beau looked agonized, out of it. He barely said hello when I walked in. I kissed him and asked what was wrong. He lifted his hands barely a fraction of an inch, shook his head slightly, then rasped, "I don't know." I suggested he get out of bed, but he resisted. "You have to," I told him. "It's a beautiful day. Let's go sit on the porch."

It took forever to get him up. He could hardly move—he was clearly in pain and anxious because he had so little motor function in his arms. I carried him gently down the steps, ferrying him more like a young son than an older brother, gliding past Mom and Dad to French doors that opened onto the front porch and looked out over a pond. We sat in chairs set right inside the open doors, just the two of us.

I didn't say much except to tell him it was going to be okay, that this is what the doctors told us would happen, that injecting the virus would cause a firestorm in his brain before it started to work and the white cells attacked the tumor. I told him it was temporary, that he just had to make it through this rough patch before things turned around. Again, he nodded his head just a bit. I could tell he was listening intently and wanted to believe everything I said.

I don't know how many minutes passed without either of us saying a word. But at some point, Beau seemed to point at a new watch I was wearing. It took me a minute to grasp what I thought he was getting at. One night when Beau was maybe fifteen, before a high school dance, he sneaked into Dad's keepsake box in the top drawer of his walk-in closet. There he found a pair of stainless steel cuff links and a 1960s Omega watch, with a leather strap, that Beau believed our Dad had been given by our mommy, the term we both used into adulthood for our mother, Neilia (we called Jill, our stepmother, "mom").

He thought the watch was so cool. So he wore it that night, without asking Dad. He planned to put it back in the box when he returned home, but he somehow lost it at the dance, to his eternal regret. He never told Dad, and Dad didn't even notice it was missing until long after. I'd forgotten all about it. But Beau remembered. He felt guilty about losing that watch forever.

Decades later, as we sat together during one of his endless-seeming hospital visits, Beau started searching for another watch to replace it. Finding a replica became an obsession for him during those months when we spent so much time waiting around—at doctors' appointments for tests and scans, in airports waiting for flights. He and I hunted everywhere, with no success. We looked online on our phones, scrolling through thousands of pictures. It was a way for us to pass the time and focus on something else entirely. I didn't even remember what the damn thing looked like, but Beau did. He recalled it exactly.

Now he seemed to gesture at my wrist. The watch I wore was an Omega Seamaster, with a metal band. I'd bought it for Beau at some point but knew he wouldn't wear it. Now it looked like he wondered why I'd gotten it—it wasn't the one we were looking for. I laughed. It was so comforting to see Beau firing enough to make an offhand observation that had nothing to do with how awful he felt.

We settled into another long, serene silence. We stared out at the landscape that unfurled before us—the green and gold of the Brandywine Valley in all its fresh spring glory, the glassy pond, the colossal red oak believed to be the oldest in the state.

Beau finally turned to me, his voice barely audible.

"Not the watch," he whispered, indicating that my Omega wasn't what he had pointed to earlier. Instead, he had been trying to point past me, at the panorama in front of us, but couldn't lift his hand high enough.

"Beautiful," he said now, nodding toward the landscape. "Beautiful . . ."

They were the last words my brother ever gave me.

I carried Beau back upstairs, slipped him into his bed, propped up his pillows, kissed him. I told him I'd be back in the morning.

Before then, however, I got another call: agitated and excruciatingly uncomfortable, he'd been taken by ambulance back to Thomas

Jefferson in Philly, where my sister Ashley's husband, Howard Krein, is a surgeon. Beau's condition wasn't getting significantly worse, but he wasn't getting better, either. A few days later, he was transferred to Walter Reed, with the hope that some rehab might help him to improve.

When I walked into his room there, Beau was clearly suffering; he clutched his abdomen in utter noncommunicative agony. It seemed to take forever to get hospital personnel to respond. As he was going septic, almost dying right then, he underwent surgery for a perforated bowel. They soon moved him to the neurological ICU, where doctors eventually decided to intubate him.

A little more than a month had passed since our time together in Houston, yet it felt like a lifetime ago. I planted myself in the chair beside Beau's bed. His wife, Hallie, camped out in the room that was cleared for her next door. She'd go to sleep there around midnight, be back up at 5 a.m.

Beau's tracheostomy tube was removed after doctors told us they'd determined recovery was no longer possible, and we waited.

Time slid by. Beau didn't stir. I kept talking. I told him it was okay to let go now. I told him that his children, Natalie, almost eleven, and Hunter, nine, would be fine, that they had the whole Biden clan there to look after them, just as we did when Mommy and Caspy left us when we were so young.

I told him Dad would be okay, too.

"He's so strong, Beau," I said. "He knows he has to be strong for all of us."

I promised him I would stay strong as well; he'd gone with me to my first AA meetings, found my first sponsor, and escorted me to rehab enough times to know what a tall order that was. I promised him I would stay sober. I promised I would take care of the family as he always had. I promised I would be happy and live the beautiful life we imagined together.

I had no idea then how many dead-end detours I'd take before I could finally keep those promises.

The twenty-four Bidens still roamed the halls. Some had gone home to shower or change or catch a quick nap, then hustled right back. Others dropped into Beau's room, said their own words to him, or conferred with the dozen or so doctors and nurses and staff who'd been so kind to us through it all.

Beau continued to breathe barely perceptible breaths. I kept holding his hand.

My aunt Val and uncle Jim, Dad's sister and brother, who practically raised Beau and me after the fatal car crash, came in and told me to get some fresh air, take a break, go for a walk. I declined. I didn't want to be anywhere but beside my brother.

Finally, almost a day and a half after doctors had given Beau hours to live, Dad insisted I go with my brother-in-law Howard to pick up some pizza. The Bidens were hungry. I feared what might happen but went anyway. Ten minutes later, as we stepped inside the restaurant, my phone buzzed. It was Dad.

"Come back, honey" was all he said.

The family was crowded inside the room along with friends and doctors and nurses. Dad stood over Beau, holding his oldest son's left hand in both of his and pressing it against his chest. My mother was beside him, while Hallie and her children huddled tearfully nearby. The lights were off, but the early evening's last rays of sun slipped through half-open shades.

The heart monitor fell still. Dr. Kevin O'Connor, Dad's White House doctor, stepped forward and solemnly announced time of death:

"Seven thirty-four p.m."

The sea of loved ones that surrounded Beau—his kids, my three daughters, our wives, in-laws, a small colony of aunts and uncles and cousins—parted to form a narrow lane for me. I stepped through the opening straight to Beau. I took his right hand, across the bed from my dad. I pressed my cheek against my brother's forehead, then kissed it. I reached out for my dad's hand as it still held Beau's. I bent and rested my head on my brother's chest and wept. Dad ran his fingers through my hair and wept with me. He then bent down to put his head close to mine and we cried together even more.

No words. Our sobs were the only sounds I heard.

Then, amid this unbearable despair, I felt my brother's chest expand just slightly. Next, I felt a heartbeat. I looked up at Dad, his eyes raw and red, and whispered, "He's still breathing." I turned to the doctors to say the same thing. They looked back at me with a mixture of concern and pity. One responded gently, "No, Hunter, I'm sorry, but your brother is—"

The heart monitor interrupted him. It started back up. No one else in the room really reacted; I'm not sure most of them recognized what was happening, they were so lost in their grief.

Understand, I didn't think Beau had miraculously recovered. I believed he'd come back for only a moment—as if he'd forgotten his wallet or his car keys—so that we both could move on. He'd returned long enough for me to tell him what he already knew, and what I'd already said, just once more.

That I loved him. That I would always be with him. That nothing could ever separate us, not even death.

Then he took a last shallow breath, and left for good.

Dr. O'Connor pronounced the time of death once more:

"Seven fifty-one p.m."

CHAPTER TWO

REQUIEM

We buried Beau seven days later.

Mourners sat shoulder to shoulder inside St. Anthony of Padua Roman Catholic Church, in Wilmington's Little Italy. The church was built by its parishioners, many of them recent immigrants and highly skilled artisans, and the main building's last stone was set down in 1926. St. Joseph on the Brandywine, our home church, built a mile away by local powder-mill workers, wasn't big enough to accommodate everyone. Yet even at St. Anthony's, guests were herded into an overflow room.

Among those attending: President Barack Obama and his family; Bill and Hillary Clinton; former attorney general Eric Holder; and Senator John McCain, who would die three years later from the same cancer that took Beau.

Army chief of staff General Raymond Odierno, the top U.S. commander in Iraq during the time Beau served there, presented my brother with a posthumous Legion of Merit medal. Chris Martin of Coldplay, one of Natalie and little Hunter's favorite musicians, performed the band's "'Til Kingdom Come." The only accompaniment as he sang alone and played acoustic guitar on the altar: the church pipe organ.

Thousands more had paid their respects at public visitations during the previous two days. The first was held at the state capital, in Dover, where Beau's flag-draped casket rested inside the Legislative Hall. The second was inside St. Anthony's. Lines snaked for blocks around each building while my family and I stood for hours without a break at each location—the only way we could meet with everyone. We hugged, held hands, and listened to memory after memory of Beau and the meaning that he'd given to people's lives.

The crowds represented all of Delaware and beyond: white, Black, brown; Italian, Irish, Polish, Jewish, Puerto Rican, Greek. Some came swaddled and cradled in their parents' arms, others were wheeled in by their adult children and caregivers.

The throngs included everybody, it sometimes seemed, that Dad, Beau, or I had ever gone to school with, worked with, or campaigned with. There were folks we'd bumped into regularly on the street or who had served us a blue plate special at a local restaurant. There were barbers who'd given Beau and me our first haircuts. There were pediatricians who'd given us physicals and dentists who'd put on our braces. There were nurses who'd worked at St. Francis Hospital from the day we were born to the day I broke my wrist for the third time, playing football my freshman year of high school.

There were teachers and teamsters, longshoremen and auto-workers, state senators and city council members. There was a woman, now in her nineties, who had supported Dad when almost no one else did at the beginning of his quixotic first run for the U.S. Senate. There were others who'd helped with that same campaign, and then each campaign that followed, knocking on doors and passing out literature every six years for almost four decades.

There was the young worker from the state building with Down syndrome whom Beau had stopped to talk with every day. There was the family of the guy who captivated Beau and me every summer at the asbestos workers' union picnic by gulping down a live cricket (I still have no idea why). There were the people whom Beau became close to while he accompanied me to AA meetings; they came because they were Beau's good friends, not because he was my brother.

Virtually everyone who shuffled and sniffled through those receiving lines had a personal story to tell or affection to pass on.

Most touching to me were the words from folks I recognized but couldn't quite place. They'd recount stories of how our families' lives intersected in such unlikely and profound ways, often with my dad at the center.

One man told me how Dad had once picked him up hitchhiking on the side of the road at midnight when he'd run out of gas. A woman remembered how Dad had called her after a death in her family, just to give his condolences. She wanted to repay his consideration. A married couple was still moved by the memory of Dad talking to them after they'd lost a son to a drunk driving accident, and they told how his words continued to give them hope and the will to go on.

The outpouring reaffirmed the singular bond born of the public tragedy of my mother's and sister's death. The consequences of that crash impacted the entire state. Republican, Democrat—it didn't matter. Delaware's residents placed their sorrows and their hopes in a dashing young widower suddenly left with two toddlers. Our survival became a source of statewide pride. Beau and I became everyone's cousins, nephews, adopted children.

Now Beau's death at so young an age, before he could fulfill his immense promise, became another call for them to huddle around us and provide whatever comfort they could.

I can't even count the number of prayer cards and medals that were pressed into my hands, each accompanied by an explanation or a directive. One older woman gave me a medal for Saint Bartholomew, who she said was the patron saint of taking the place of another. "You have to carry your brother's life forward," she told me, her grip tightening. It was a recurring sentiment. (I later learned Bartholomew is also the patron saint of butchers, bookbinders, leather workers, and those afflicted with nervous disorders.)

Then there were the families who told us how Beau had counseled them while prosecuting sex crimes, a priority during his eight years as state attorney general. That focus was highlighted by the horrific case of serial child molester Earl Brian Bradley, a pediatrician who violated more than one hundred children, including a three-month-old. Beau took the case so personally that it was one reason he declined to run for my father's former seat in the U.S. Senate in 2010. He was determined to pursue Bradley's prosecution on what grew to more than five hundred counts.

On June 23, 2011, Bradley was convicted on all counts, then sentenced to fourteen consecutive life prison terms—plus another 164 years—without parole.

Yet Beau's reach in that area extended far beyond the courtroom. A longtime friend of ours, a tough forty-something union guy, came up to me and confided, "Your brother made it possible for me to think about not killing myself."

I asked him, gently, what he was talking about. He stood stunned for a moment, believing that Beau surely had disclosed his story to me. He then related how he'd been molested repeatedly by a priest thirty-five years earlier. The priest had since died, but Beau was the only person he'd ever told. The guy knew what everybody else who'd ever confided in Beau knew: he could be trusted with anyone's deepest, darkest secrets, and he would never judge them.

Talking with all those people in those receiving lines provided me and the rest of my family with an incredible uplift at the most awful time. If ever there was a question about the impact of a life well-lived, it was answered, loud and clear, by the legions who poured past Beau's casket during those two days.

Our family did what our family always does in a crisis, whether it's political or personal: everybody took a role.

Dad and I dealt with parts of the planning together, from making decisions about who would speak at the service and when to fielding the calls of dignitaries from all over the world. Dad sat on his porch for hours and took one call after another from current and former leaders from every hemisphere and every country. They all had affection for him; not just respect, but true affection. So each conversation became more than just passing along condolences. It included a story about when "you brought Beau and Hunter to Berlin," or how "I was so impressed with Beau when he came back to speak about corruption in Romania when he was attorney general," or "I don't know if you remember when my niece died, but you were there for our family."

Most of the time I was encamped at Beau's house in Wilmington, less than a mile from Dad's. I handled condolences and well-wishers there and greeted friends who stopped by to see Hallie and her kids.

Our time became so swallowed up or interrupted by others that Dad and I never really sat together to have a heart-to-heart, to talk about what we were going through. We both cried a lot—I saw Dad cry, on his porch, after almost every call. There were moments when we simply held each other, as if holding each other up, soundlessly, realizing it was all we could do, that there were no words to take away the pain. Words almost felt risky. I was scared to death of what Beau's passing was going to do to him, and he was scared to death of what it was going to do to me.

Each of us, in our way, dreaded the impending doom.

In the midst of it all, I worked on Beau's eulogy. The thought of writing it amplified the emotions I'd been experiencing, and the prospect of delivering it to such a large, divergent audience only made Beau's loss more acute.

Yet once I began, those concerns receded and then blew clean away. Despite the enormity of this public address, I realized I was preparing it for an audience of one: my brother. Hell, I knew he'd be fine with anything I came up with—again, that was Beau. So I would write passages and read them back to him aloud. He and I would then edit them and hone them together—at least that's how it felt. I was amazed at how easily it all came.

I went through a number of significant milestones in our lives, beginning with where it always began: waking up to him in the hospital. I wanted everyone else to understand the immensity of our connection, but I also felt a responsibility to recognize just how many others claimed an enormous connection to my brother as well. The personal responses we received that week underscored that.

Writing his eulogy was at once heart-wrenching and cathartic. That's the effect I hoped it would have on others. That's the effect I hoped it would have on our dad.

When I finished, I didn't read it to Dad. I wanted him to hear it for the first time inside St Anthony's.

The first eulogy was delivered by General Odierno, his chest blooming with medals. He spoke to Beau's character and selflessness while serving in Iraq, and then about his moral and ethical roots while serving as the state's attorney general. He brought up Beau's "natural charisma" and how others, soldiers and civilians alike, "willingly wanted to follow him."

He then voiced a sentiment expressed by practically everyone who ever met Beau.

"He was committed to his community, to his home state," the four-star general emphasized, "and to a nation that I believed one day Beau Biden would lead."

When he finished, General Odierno stepped before Beau's casket, stood ramrod still for a long moment, then honored it with a slow, deliberate salute.

President Obama followed. Framed by an altar splashed with white roses and hydrangeas and backlit by the soft glow pouring through the sanctuary's rose window, the president eulogized Beau for nearly twenty-five minutes. He spoke from notes with the same calm solemnity that had carried him through the last seven long years. He made even those relegated to the overflow room feel as if he were speaking directly to them.

So much of his eulogy, however, was directed at my father, even referring to him at one point as a "brother."

Beau and I admired the president immensely, not only for the way he treated our dad but for the way he treated our family. (He was my president first and foremost, and he was also my daughter Maisy's basketball coach.) But it was complicated, though none of that was going through my mind right then. The infighting and internal politicking natural to any White House sometimes spilled over to my dad. I took it personally—maybe too personally—whenever I learned that some aide in the administration had tried to undercut him. So I didn't hang around the White House much; I didn't want to be in the position of walking into a barbecue on a Sunday with the president and the White House staff after reading about someone throwing my dad under the bus. I knew I couldn't control my temper and keep my mouth shut.

Kathleen, however, had become close with Michelle Obama, and our daughter Maisy and her daughter Sasha had been good pals since the second grade at Sidwell Friends, where they both went to school. Kathleen and Michelle worked out together at the gym and often had evening cocktails at the White House, at both formal and informal events. I had relapsed two years after the election and didn't feel comfortable around that scene at all, and often got the impression that there were people who didn't feel comfortable around me.

But Beau's service was personal and not political, and the president was all in that morning for my dad, my brother, and the rest of our family. I was nothing but appreciative.

The president opened by quoting the Irish poet Patrick Kavanagh: "'A man is original when he speaks the truth that has always been known to all good men.'" Beau, he then said rightly, was an original, "A man who loved deeply, and was loved in return."

He talked of the accident that took our mother and sister, and how it shaped Beau's life—all of our lives.

"For Beau, a cruel twist of fate came early," he said. "But Beau was a Biden. And he learned early the Biden family rule: if you have to ask for help, it's too late. It meant you were never alone; you don't even have to ask, because someone is always there for you when you need them."

The president noted my dad's tender yet purposeful reaction after that tragedy, how he carried on in public service (Mike Mansfield, longest-serving majority leader in the history of the Senate, convinced Dad not to resign the office during those days between the crash and taking the oath), how he eschewed "the parlor games of Washington" and instead commuted home to Wilmington every day to see us kids off to school and kiss us good night.

"As Joe himself confessed to me," the president put in, "he did not just do this because the kids needed him. He did it because he needed those kids."

President Obama followed that with a litany of Beau's many accomplishments, calling him "a soldier who dodged glory," a prosecutor "who defended the defenseless," and that "rare politician who collected more fans than foes."

He summed him up, to appreciative laughter: "He even looked and sounded like Joe, although I think Joe would be the first to acknowledge that Beau was an upgrade—Joe 2.0."

"Beau was . . . someone who charmed you, and disarmed you, put you at ease," the president continued, providing a lighthearted inventory into the essence of both the public and the private Beau. "When he'd have to attend a fancy fundraiser with people who took themselves way too seriously, he'd walk over to you and whisper something wildly inappropriate in your ear. The son of a senator, a major in the Army, the most popular elected official in Delaware— I'm sorry, Joe—but he was not above dancing in nothing but a sombrero and shorts at Thanksgiving if it would shake loose a laugh from the people he loved.

"And through it all, he was the consummate public servant, a notebook in his back pocket at all times so he could write down the problems of everyone he met and go back to the office and get them fixed.

"This was a man who, at the Democratic National Convention, didn't spend all his time in the back rooms with donors or glad-handing," he continued. "Instead, he rode the escalators in the arena with his son, up and down, up and down, again and again, knowing, just like Joe had learned, what ultimately mattered in life."

The president paused a moment before he went on, as if anticipating the political sea change that loomed around the corner. "You know, anyone can make a name for themselves in this reality-TV age, especially in today's politics. If you're loud enough or controversial enough, you can get some attention. But to make that name mean something, to have it associated with dignity and integrity—that is rare."

Near the end, the president borrowed another line from the same Irish poet he'd quoted at the start. This one encapsulated the sadness we all felt even as we smiled at Beau's bright memories:

"'And I said, let grief be a fallen leaf at the dawning of the day.'"

The president stepped down from the altar and walked over to Dad, who stood to accept a long, full embrace. The president then kissed my father on the side of his head—a gesture of the brotherhood he'd noted earlier—before finally letting go.

My sister followed the president. I accompanied her up to the altar and remained at her side, a show of sibling unity for Beau. She was funny and adoring and hopeful and poignant—the quintessential kid sister.

"When I was in first grade, I drew a picture of what made me happy," said Ashley, who was ten years Beau's junior. "And it was me holding hands with my two brothers."

She made it clear that she saw the two of us almost as one, just as Beau and I did: two sides of the same coin.

"It's impossible to talk about Beau without talking about Hunter," she said. "They were inseparable and shared a love that was unconditional. Although Beau was a year and a day older, Hunter was the wind beneath Beau's wings—Hunt gave him the courage and the confidence to fly . . . There wasn't one decision where Hunter wasn't consulted first, not one day that passed where they didn't speak, and not one road traveled where they weren't each other's copilots.

"Hunter was Beau's confidant," she said. "His home."

Ashley had quickly shared in our bond. As with any good sibling, we loved her and were annoyed by her in equal measure.

"It was true then and it remained true throughout my life—I feel like the luckiest kid sister to be raised and built by two extraordinary men," she said. "Although, as my husband sometimes points out, they didn't read all the directions."

Ashley then noted the events that passed as milestones in a kid sister's eyes, including the fact that Beau and I introduced her to her future husband, Howard, after we first met him at an Obama-Biden fundraiser in 2008.

Beau and I named Ashley when she was born, and she referred to us as Beauie and Huntie ever after. She hung around with us so much when we were in high school and college that our friends nicknamed her "flea." Beau's lone precondition for her presence: she had to sing "Fire on the Mountain" by the Grateful Dead. As an eight-year-old, she sometimes spent the night at Beau's college apartment.

Ashley recalled our annual Thanksgiving trips to Nantucket,

when "my brothers would come get me out of class and we would pile up in the Jeep Wagoneer and travel seven hours—my favorite car ride."

The past year had weighed heavily on her, just as it had on all of us, yet she, too, saw a blessing in being beside our brother during that final phase of his life. She talked about what she termed the "tragic privilege" of accompanying Beau to his chemo appointments every other Friday. Afterward, they often stopped for breakfast, during which Beau made her listen to what she came to think of as his theme song: "You Get What You Give," by the New Radicals. She repeated the lyrics for those sitting rapt in the full church.

> *This whole damn world could fall apart*
> *You'll be okay, follow your heart.*
> *You're in harm's way, I'm right behind.*

"In retrospect," Ashley said, "I think Beau played that song during our mornings together—not for him, but for me. To remember to not give up or let sadness consume me, consume us."

She then summed up:

"As long as I have Hunt, I have you. So Beauie . . . see you. Love you so much."

Ashley and I kissed and hugged. I couldn't have been prouder. I knew Beau couldn't have been prouder, either.

She'd set everyone at ease, including me. As I stepped behind the podium and opened my notes, I felt calm—uncharacteristically calm. I dread speaking in front of big crowds. I'd been aware of how much everyone worried about me, and not just at this moment. I'd sensed a general concern about the effect Beau's passing would have on my sobriety. Under other circumstances, that concern would have only heightened my anxiety.

Not now.

With a thousand faces staring up at me, and the service being watched by millions more on TV, I felt cocooned within my family: Ashley, Mom and Dad, my aunts and uncles and cousins, my wife and daughters—they all were there with me, and they all were there for me.

And then there was Beau. Since the day that he died, it still didn't feel as if Beau was gone.

After thanking the speakers who came before me, and reaffirming Beau's love for Ashley—"He loved the way you laugh. He loved your smile"—I spoke directly to Beau's children. They huddled together in the front pew. I repeated what I'd told them all week: that their father would always be with them and a part of them, and that their extended family would love and protect them the way that same family loved and protected me and their father.

"Natalie," I went on, "he is that piece of you that allows you to be so caring and compassionate. He's the reason why you are so protective of your brother, the same way he was with me.

"Hunter, Robert Hunter Biden the Second—he tied you and me together forever. You are his calm and his focus. You are so much like your daddy, you know, watching the two of you fish at the end of the dock was like seeing two images of the same person.

"Just like Aunt Valerie was there for your daddy and me—just like we had Uncle Jimmy, Uncle Frankie, Uncle Jack, Uncle John, Mom-Mom and Da-Da—you have your aunt Ashley, your aunt Liz, your aunt Kathleen, your Poppy and Mimi, your Nana and Pop. We will surround you with the same love, a love so big and so beautiful. The same love that made your daddy and me will now make you."

I had no inkling then, of course, of just how complicated all that soon would become.

I retold the story about Beau holding my hand when we were scared kids in the hospital room, and how mine was hardly the only hand he held over the years in someone's time of great need. Survivors of abuse, parents of fallen soldiers, victims of violent crime—he held them all.

"There are thousands of people telling those stories right now," I said. "Telling the same story—about when Beau Biden held their hand.

"He was clarity," I continued, speaking as much to myself as to those inside the church. "A clarity you can step into. He was the clarity of Lake Skaneateles at sunrise. A clarity you could float in. A clarity that was contagious. He was that clarity not just for his family but for everyone who called him friend.

"My only claim on my brother," I then told everyone ever touched by Beau, "is that he held my hand first."

As I read those words, time didn't exist for me anymore. I had no idea how long I'd been up there (it was twenty-two minutes at that point). I didn't worry about what anyone thought or about anyone's concerns.

"Forty-two years ago," I finally concluded, "I believe that God gave us a gift. He gave us the gift of sparing my brother, sparing him long enough to give the love of a thousand lifetimes. God gave us a boy who had no limits to the weight of love he could bear.

"And as it began, so it did end: His family surrounding him. Everyone holding on to him. Each of us desperately holding him. Each of us whispering, 'I love you. I love you. I love you.' And I held his hand as he took his last breath. I know that I was loved, and I know that his hand will never leave mine."

When I finished and returned to my pew, Dad stood to kiss me. He then whispered in my ear:

"Beautiful."

I felt hope after that long week. I even sensed that others had begun to feel hopeful about me. Standing for hours in those receiving lines, it seemed every third person I hugged or shook hands with encouraged me to move back to Delaware and run for office.

Kathleen and I drove back to Washington the morning after Beau's funeral. It was just the two of us. We listened to the radio station out of the University of Pennsylvania. Beau and I had loved it growing up. Now it was airing a three-shift tribute to Beau, a 1991 alum.

At one point, I pulled the car over and told Kathleen that maybe politics was now an option for me.

"You know, as horrible as I feel, I have a feeling of real purpose," I said. It seemed so many people were more willing to forgive my past mistakes—relapses with drinking, administrative discharge from the Navy Reserve—than I was willing to forgive myself.

But I underestimated how much the wreckage of my past and all that I put my family through still weighed on Kathleen.

I suppose her response—Are you serious?—was entirely warranted.

We didn't say another word to each other for the rest of the ride.

Or, really, ever again.

CHAPTER THREE

GROWING UP BIDEN

My father believed Beau could one day be president and that he'd get there with my help.

It seemed wholly natural. The two of us were raised on politics like farm kids raised on sweet corn. The rule Beau and I had as kids was that we could go with our dad to Washington whenever we wanted, though there was an unspoken limit to missing school too many days in a row. So two or three times a month we took the train with him to the Capitol and spent the day there. It was more like visiting the house of out-of-town relatives than being on one of those school field trips we saw all the other fidgety kids on. The people who worked for and with my father were like surrogate aunts and uncles. It wasn't unusual for someone like Bill Cohen, say, then a Republican representative from Maine and later secretary of defense under Clinton, to ride the train back to Wilmington with Dad, have dinner with us, hang out, and stay overnight.

I'd sit on Dad's lap during staff meetings, or take off with Beau to roam the Senate gym in the Russell Senate Office Building, which for us was just this big, rambling neo-Greek playground with a pool. Beau and I sometimes wandered into the steam room, where we'd find big-eared, bearlike Howell Heflin, Democratic senator from Alabama, chewing on his ever-present cigar as he shot the breeze with the youngish, still athletic-looking Ted Kennedy and an aging, angular Strom Thurmond.

They'd spot us and call out, "Hey, boys!"—we were always the only kids around—and we'd settle into some nearby corner to eavesdrop. Amid the swirling steam, the room filled with a chorus of mellifluous accents and clashing ideologies—conservative Democrat, liberal standard-bearer, rock-ribbed Republican. To our young ears, their chatter was as much music-making as politicking.

We were fixtures in the Senate cafeteria, knew all the waitstaff. Dad sat with us when he could, ordering a tuna fish on wheat and calling over whoever caught his eye. If Dad got pulled away, a senator would essentially babysit us. While I slurped navy bean soup and dug into a BLT (Beau always ordered a grilled cheese and fries), someone like Dan Inouye, from Hawaii, would share stories between bites about his Army buddies during World War II. I didn't connect those tales to the shirt and jacket sleeve he pinned to his shoulder until years later, when I wrote a thesis paper in college about the senator's heroism in leading an assault in Italy with the 442nd Infantry Regiment, the all Japanese American fighting unit, and losing his right arm to a grenade.

John Glenn, the astronaut-turned-senator from Ohio, would

spot us waiting for Dad and call out, "Okay, boys, up to my office." He'd lead us up there to show off models of his Project Mercury rocket, point to where he sat inside the *Friendship 7* spacecraft, then regale us with tales about what it was like to be the first American to spin around in space and look down on entire oceans and continents. We'd just stare, our eyes wide and mouths open.

We absorbed some lasting lessons along the way, especially from when our father was new enough to have mentors and teachable moments, Washington style. I recall him telling us about a tutorial he'd gotten not long after arriving in office from Mike Mansfield, the longtime Senate majority leader from Montana.

Jesse Helms had been elected to the Senate the same year as Dad. When the Rehabilitation Act, a precursor of the Americans with Disabilities Act, was introduced in 1973, the hard-shell conservative from North Carolina—and bearer of another one of those mellifluous accents—went on the Senate floor to excoriate it as a massive federal overreach. Dad was so disgusted afterward that he responded with his own not-so-measured rant and asked, in effect, how anyone could be so callous, uncaring, and mean-spirited as to oppose such a magnanimous and much-needed bill.

Later, Mansfield summoned Dad to his office. "Iron Mike"— quiet, courteous, unfailingly persuasive—laid down his unwritten but inviolable law: you can question a colleague's judgment, whether it be a Democrat or a Republican, but you should never question his or her motives. Everybody comes to the Senate for a reason, he went on, but nobody comes for the sole purpose of being mean-spirited or un-American. Someone's judgment might be off, but his or her motives weren't open to questioning, particularly on sensitive issues like this.

To illuminate his point, Mansfield told Dad a story about Helms. Several years earlier, Jesse and his wife, Dot, who'd been married for twenty years and were the parents of two teenage daughters, woke one morning around Christmas and read a newspaper article about a nine-year-old orphan with cerebral palsy. In the story, the boy, who used a wheelchair, said that all he wanted for Christmas was a mother and a father and a real home. Jesse and Dot decided right then, Mansfield's story went, to adopt him and bring him into their family.

"You can question his judgment," Mansfield then reiterated to Dad, "but certainly you can see how you shouldn't question his motive."

Dad swiftly learned that if he didn't put an opponent's character front and center, he often could find a way to change minds or work out a compromise. No one walks out of a meeting when you say, "I don't think you understand the ramifications of what you're doing, how people won't have access to things they need in their daily lives." That prompts debate. But if you tell an opponent, "You're just a mean-spirited jackass who's clearly prejudiced against people with disabilities"—well, if you're Jesse Helms, or anyone else for that matter, the conversation is over.

That lesson, long a foundational one for my dad and our family, is one that too many politicians today have failed to pick up. The result is the toxic atmosphere that blew the door wide open for somebody like Trump, who has since turned that lesson on its head.

Trump's motives can and should be questioned because, hell, most of the time he flat-out states them. And take my word, those motives ain't pretty.

Having been around the Senate since I was three years old, I've watched the evolution of the people who've come into that chamber as conservative firebrands and later voted for liberal-backed issues not because they changed ideology, but because it was the right thing to do—like marking Martin Luther King Jr. Day as a national holiday, as Strom Thurmond eventually did, or supporting an extension of the Voting Rights Act, as did John Stennis, as staunch a Mississippi segregationist as there was.

Even Jesse Helms, who'd once declared AIDS "God's punishment for homosexuals," supported funding for AIDS relief in Africa during his last years in office.

Men and women can come to the Senate with one view of the world, but it's difficult to stay in that office for any length of time and not be exposed to more diverse viewpoints and ways to arrive at judgments—at least, it was, before the fearmongering cult of Trumpism. It's hard not to turn more empathetic. Most longtime political observers think those days of bipartisanship are gone for good. I hope it's not true. Jeff Flake came to the Senate as Arizona's right-wing counterpart to John McCain, and look at him now: a confirmed never-Trumper.

In the midst of the political storm that swirls around me, I try to stay optimistic. I'm not always successful. I'll glance up at a TV in the middle of the day and see Lindsey Graham, a man from the opposite side of the aisle whom my dad and family have long considered a friend, morph into a Trump lapdog right before my eyes, slandering me and my father in the coldest, most cynical, most self-serving ways.

Beau and I didn't grow up in Washington. We didn't really hang out with other senators' kids. Especially in those early days, we took the hour-and-a-half train ride with our dad from Wilmington to the Russell Building and back again, and that was pretty much it—the extent of our Washington upbringing.

Home was Delaware. That's where politics formed us and made it possible for us to get to know the entire state like the backs of our hands. Delaware is often viewed as an irrelevant blip by many who aren't from there, and for obvious reasons: With not quite a million residents, it's the sixth smallest state in the country in population, and it's the second-smallest state in area, behind only teeny Rhode Island. It's easy to miss on a map if you're not looking for it, squeezed as it is between Pennsylvania, Maryland, and New Jersey.

Yet Delaware is an overlooked, underappreciated microcosm of America and a key contributor to my dad's broad national appeal. The state's history, culture, and politics reflect aspects associated with bigger distinct regions. It is at once a Northeastern suburb of Philadelphia; a cradle of Southern agriculture and race relations; a slice of the industrial Midwest; and a watery, port-centric belt like so many other areas up and down the mid-Atlantic.

The state's North-South friction is longstanding and complex. Delaware was a slave state that never left the Union, with most of its citizenry taking up arms against the Confederacy. It was a cross-roads for the Underground Railroad, with freed slaves outnumbering those still in bondage ten to one. Yet despite being the first of the original thirteen colonies to ratify the Constitution, it was the last one where slavery remained legal.

There's a vibrant African American community in Wilmington, whose population of just over seventy thousand has one of the highest percentages of Black residents per capita in the country. Louis Redding, the first African American admitted to the Delaware bar, was part of the legal team that challenged school segregation in *Brown v. Board of Education*. The city exploded in pent-up anger in the 1960s, and preachers in the city's Black churches forged strong bonds during the civil rights movement with Black preachers in the Deep South.

Wilmington's historically high voter turnout in 1972 was perhaps the biggest reason—along with my mother's political instincts—that Dad won his Senate seat. There was the conviction in the Black community, which still holds true there and beyond, that "Joe is our guy."

Though the differences might not be as stark as they once were, the state remains divided north and south, or upper and lower, by the Chesapeake & Delaware Canal. The upper portion views itself as more sophisticated, an adjunct of Philly and the Northeast corridor. It's where 60 percent of all Fortune 500 companies are incorporated, due in large part to the state's long-standing Court of Chancery, a special judicial body that rules on corporate law disputes expediently and without juries.

It's also an area long dominated by the du Pont family, whose wealth afforded them a tight grip on local industry and politics. With a fortune that originated in gunpowder and explosives, then expanded into chemicals and cars, the du Ponts dominated the state's political landscape throughout the nineteenth and twentieth centuries.

The family also owned a controlling stake in General Motors from 1917 until 1957, when the U.S. Supreme Court ordered it to divest its shares, saying its control created a monopoly that interfered with the free flow of commerce. One lasting sign of the family's passion for cars: the DuPont Highway (U.S. Routes 13 and 113), which parallels the top of the state to the bottom, was built by T. Coleman du Pont to improve transportation for farmers and other businesses within Delaware. It also gave him a smooth, unimpeded road on which to enjoy his long Sunday drives.

The lower part of the state has traditionally been more rural, white, and Southern. If you grew up in Sussex County, you simply said you were from "below the canal." Farmers there raise corn, soy, and broiler chickens, which outnumber the state's residents by about 200 to 1.

Beau and I saw all of it. Union halls and Democratic Party picnics were as much a part of our growing up as tree forts and sleepovers. Before we could walk, our mommy toted us around in picnic baskets to rallies and meet-and-greets and door-knocking campaigns in a state where you could almost literally rap on every door. As we got older, Beau and I stood inside the Bethel African Methodist Episcopal Church in Wilmington, waiting as Sunday services let out so we could shake hands with Black parishioners streaming out of the stone church's big red doors. We tagged along with Dad to rural Kent County, dropping in on people whose families had owned the same chicken farms for a hundred years. We'd drive farther south, into Sussex County, where Beau and I would bid each other up on a coconut cream pie (Dad's favorite) in auctions held for churches or school fundraisers. Sometimes we were the only bidders.

While most Southerners consider Delaware to be Northern, a community like Gumboro, near the Great Cypress Swamp and host each year to the Gumboro Mud Bog, is every bit as Southern as a small town in Georgia.

Given that diverse crucible, it's easy to trace my dad's, and later Beau's, seemingly innate political ability to relate with people of all backgrounds, races, and ideological leanings. Growing up in Delaware doesn't mean you're automatically aware of what a microcosm it is. But when you grow up in Delaware the son of Joe Biden, you have no choice. You not only learn how to get along with all kinds of people, you come to understand what motivates them, what they care about, and what they really need.

That's the state that adopted Beau and me when our mother died.

Beau and I never really grieved the loss of our mother and baby sister.

We never thought it was something we had to grieve.

This was in part, of course, because we were so young. But more than that, it was because of our father's heroic marshaling of family to surround and enfold us in uninterrupted love.

Beau and I talked about that often as we got older—how lucky we were despite the tragedy. We were almost ashamed to admit to any sadness we might have felt because of how enveloped we were in that familial embrace. It almost felt like a betrayal to say that we missed our mom when, nearly from the moment we left the hospital, we had my dad's sister—Aunt Val—move in and not only take care of our immediate daily needs but also be as warm and tender and emotive as a mother figure could possibly be. My dad's brother Uncle Jimmy converted our garage into an apartment so that he could be a constant presence in our lives. We were also tended to by our many other uncles and aunts, as well as by our grandparents—I still remember my grandmother making me feel better simply with a soft hand on my face, or scratching my back in bed, or warming up a bowl of her homemade beef-vegetable soup.

I don't think I've ever fully come to terms with the violence of the actual incident, regardless of whether I've conjured it in my mind's eye as an actual memory or if it remains buried in my subconscious. The fact is, it exists: it happened, and Beau and I were there.

The one thing he and I never asked each other was this: "What do you remember?" I don't know why. I don't know if it even occurred to either of us to ask.

I think we both absorbed that day and its aftermath in similar ways, but the effects manifested themselves differently in each of us. I really believe that its trauma and stress contributed to my brother's health problems. He kept so much of it locked inside, and I can't help but think it eventually took a toll, no matter how positively he always viewed things.

As for me, I want to make it clear: I don't see that tragic moment as necessarily resulting in behaviors that lent themselves to addiction. That would be a cop-out. But I do have a better understanding of why I feel the way I do sometimes, the unease I've experienced at incongruous moments, especially around other people—at social gatherings, political functions, random encounters in a school or at an airport or during a meeting. It was a lonely place to be as a child, and it's a lonely place to be now. That kind of insecurity is almost universal among those with real addiction issues—a feeling of being alone in a crowd.

I've always felt alone in a crowd.

Yet while we didn't talk about it as kids, I was hyperaware of my mommy's death—and hyperaware of her absence. I loved hearing relatives' stories about her, holding tight to their portrayals of how special she was, how tough she was, how compassionate she was. They described her to me as smart, decisive, beautiful. The word I heard most often was "elegant," as it related both to her demeanor and her physical appearance. She came across as something close to regal yet eminently approachable. She was loyal almost to a fault, an incredible politician in her own right, and an unflinching force behind Dad's rise in Washington at the absurdly young age of twenty-nine.

I was not consciously aware, however, of how much her loss represented a missing piece of the family puzzle. While that hole was filled with something very special, what was lost was never recovered. It was as if someone had torn a section from a painting and replaced it with a lovely likeness. Our family remained a beautiful if reconfigured composition, one that was born out of tragedy and rearranged by an overwhelming desire to make sure that Beau and I were okay. Yet for me, that original piece was always missing, always gone.

When our dad remarried five years after "the accident," as we called it, he gave us the bonus of the Mom we have now ("When are 'we' going to get married?" Beau and I would pester Dad, constantly encouraging him to propose). A high school teacher from Willow Grove, Pennsylvania, Jill Biden did an amazing job of taking over the role of our mom—with a curious public looking on. I consider her to be my mother as much as one can possibly imagine.

Yet I still longed for what was lost, even if I couldn't quite remember it.

It has taken me more than forty years to acknowledge that original loss, address that original trauma, recognize that original pain. And it has taken that long for me to understand that my doing so isn't a betrayal of those who tried their mightiest to save Beau and me from the worst of it.

I remember my childhood as almost idyllic. I spent most of my time riding BMX bikes with Beau on back roads all over the outskirts of Wilmington, or hiking along railroad tracks and building forts in the woods.

Other times we headed to Buck Road to throw acorns at cars. Beau and I and another friend followed a disciplined set of rules: Never throw at a car driven by a woman or an elderly person. The highest-value target was a teenager in a van, but we basically zeroed in on people we knew would stop and chase us. We had places all along the road where we could best chuck the acorns and then hide. It was horribly stupid and we freaking loved it.

Some days we hung out at a little convenience store and used the money we made cutting lawns to buy Cokes, hot dogs, and candy bars, and then played video games—*Centipede*, *Space Invaders*—until we drove the clerks crazy and they ran us out. We'd bike over to the Gulf station and clean customers' windshields for tips until we drove the owner there crazy, too. We'd then head over to Gandalf's, a video-rental store in a strip mall, and poke through videos until we could sneak into the X-rated section tucked away in the back.

When we were home, we played one-on-one basketball or football for hours, beating the living shit out of each other. Our buddies came over on weekends to play pickup games; in the winter, we played hockey on the pond behind our house. When we all got bored enough, BB-gun wars broke out.

Because our birthdays fell just a day apart, Beau and I celebrated them together, alternating the day we held it on: February 3 one year, February 4 the next. The whole extended family—aunts, uncles, cousins—showed up to celebrate. We alternated the dinner we served, too: for me, chicken pot pie that Mom made from scratch; for Beau, spaghetti and meatballs. But when it came time to blow out the candles, every year there was a vanilla cake with chocolate icing for me and brownies (with candles) for Beau.

Those massive family gatherings at our house were repeated every year at a Christmas Eve dinner—all of it on behalf of my brother and me, all of it to keep us whole. I grew up watching, without always fully appreciating, my entire family perform the most selfless deeds on our behalf, without any real benefit to themselves. Everyone took a turn as a hero in our story; everyone performed a kind of magic act. It was an obvious expression of how much they loved my dad, who understood something rare, something truly genius: trauma gave us the gift of each other.

Beau always saw that his role as older brother included being my protector. He and our mom joked around together all the time, sometimes directing their humor at me, all in good fun. I was more sensitive, or maybe just less mature, and was as often confused by their jokes as I was in on them. My new mom was doing a great job, especially with everyone watching. Although she showed her deep love for me in ways I only fully understood later—her steadfast and undying loyalty, as just one example—the rhythms and dynamics of our new home were now slightly different. I was confused by that. I started to act out at school, not in alarming ways, just small, silly rebellions.

Between third and fourth grade, I transferred from Quaker-run Wilmington Friends to St. Edmond's Academy, an all-boys Catholic school. Beau was moving that year from the Lower School at Friends to the Upper School across the street, so we wouldn't be in the same building anyway. I don't recall exactly why I wanted to transfer; again, I was probably being overly sensitive. My best friend at Wilmington Friends had cystic fibrosis, a boy named David who everyone was certain wouldn't make it past the age of eighteen. I'd stay inside with him while he took his medicine during recess, after which a teacher gave each of us a Tootsie Roll. We'd head outside for the last few minutes of freedom, and some kids there teased us mercilessly.

I didn't fare much better at St. Edmond's. I think I still hold the record for most demerits. In fifth grade, I once asked to be excused to go to the bathroom, where I met up with two friends. We started horsing around, throwing toilet paper at each other and standing on top of the stalls while we urinated. Mr. Fox, a teacher I couldn't stand, walked in and hit the roof. I knew I'd be in big trouble at home, so I decided to run away.

I also knew Beau would be devastated if I left him. So I wrote him a letter that was as melodramatic as it was sincere.

Dear Beau, it began, *I love you more than anything in the world but I can't stay here anymore. I'll come back and find you but now I have to go. Please don't look for me.*

I then hid under my bed. A little later I heard Beau crying, telling our mom between sobs that she was the reason I took off. Dad called and Mom told him that she and Beau were going out to search for me. After they left, I slinked outside and climbed a tree in the yard. I stayed up there even after Beau and Mom returned home. Beau was still devastated, which actually made me feel better, seeing how much my brother missed me. I was like Tom Sawyer attending his own funeral.

Then my dad came home. I didn't know what to do. I couldn't hide in the tree all night. I finally clambered down and went inside, prepared for the worst. But everybody was just ecstatic to see me, safe and unharmed.

Also, it turned out, Mom told me that she wasn't all that fond of Mr. Fox, either. I loved her for that.

I transferred back to Friends the next year.

Another kind of education took place most nights around our dinner table. It's hard to think of anything of political significance over the course of my life that Dad wasn't a part of. One result: we had a catbird seat to history from the perspective of one of its central players. When big issues were brought up while we ate—arms control with the Soviet Union, economic sanctions against South Africa—it was almost always in the context of, "What's the plan, Dad? What are you going to do?"

Beau and I loved his elaborate talks about current events, usually beginning with historical backgrounding that could reach back centuries, then ending with the personalities and dynamics at play today.

The day-to-day politics of Washington—the battle lines drawn around the major policy and legislative fights—was a constant conversation because it had an impact on our father's career, which was something that my brother and I became intimately involved in. We both wanted him to run for president every time he could. We'd give him a million reasons why he would win, which wasn't always the most dispassionate advice: it was coming from sons who thought their father walked on water.

His primary campaign for the Democratic nomination for president in 1987, while we were teenagers, ended shortly after it began. We were devastated. He was accused of plagiarism when he loosely appropriated parts of a speech given by Neil Kinnock, the British

Labour Party leader, without citing him. In fact, Dad had cited Kinnock in a dozen other speeches. It was a distorted political hit job that stuck in that pre-Clinton era when a single smear could sink a campaign. In today's environment, it would hardly be a blip.

It was awful for Beau and me to watch the man we idolized be publicly humiliated on such a grand scale. I even tried to punch out some hecklers who taunted Dad at a Penn lightweight-football game that Beau was playing in until Beau's buddies jumped in to break it up. While the campaign's demise clearly weighed on him, Dad didn't break a sweat, from what we could see. He dropped out that September, then did what he always does in the face of adversity: put his head down and went back to work.

We were senator's sons yet staunchly middle-class. We had a beautiful house in Wilmington that had once been owned by a du Pont, but it needed a ton of work. Dad closed off half of it with drywall every winter because we couldn't afford to heat the whole thing. He pulled on a hazmat suit to scrape asbestos off the basement pipes himself. Dad, Beau, and I painted one side of the house every summer; when I was younger, Dad dangled me by the ankles from the third-floor windows to slap paint under the eaves. By the time all four sides were finished, the front needed to be painted again and we started all over. We planted six-foot mature cypress trees around the four-acre yard for a hedge. If Beau and I didn't finish cutting the lawn over the weekend, we'd come home late from school and see Dad on a riding mower, in the dark, lights on, rolling up and down until it was done.

I started working at age eleven mowing lawns in the neighborhood with Beau, and there wasn't a summer we weren't required to have a job. My first legal-age employment was at the Brandywine Zoo. I shoveled piles of llama manure as tall as I was and unclogged the drain in the otter pool, where I sometimes became part of the attraction as visitors watched through a glass window as the otters attacked me.

Beau and I also worked for a cold-storage company. We started out in the inspection room, where a USDA guy plucked six random boxes from a railcar filled with sixty-pound hunks of frozen beef shipped from Australia and New Zealand. We'd slice off a big slab with a table saw, wrap it in plastic, thaw it in a vat of near-boiling water, then lay it out for the inspector.

From there, we progressed in different directions.

Beau became a dock manager—the guy in the hard hat and white lab coat who toted a clipboard as he marked shipments headed for the deep freeze and had the pallet drivers sign paperwork. He worked from 8 a.m. to 4 p.m. and never got his nails dirty. He worked desk jobs all through college.

I unloaded the sixty-pound boxes from railcars filled from floor to ceiling, often working from 6 a.m. to 10 p.m. It paid better and you earned overtime. I also worked at a local restaurant in Greenville, Delaware, as a waiter before being demoted to busboy, after which I was demoted to dishwasher. Later, I parked cars for a valet company and pushed a cart through the Senate office buildings to deliver photos taken with visitors.

Beau clearly made smarter choices right from the start.

In high school, Beau became known as "the sheriff." Not only was he the designated driver, he was also the designated leader. Parents knew that as long as their kids were with Beau, they were safe. He would disqualify friends from a party because they drank too much; if Beau told you to stop drinking, you stopped drinking. He was the sole arbiter and everybody respected that. But he didn't act like everybody's mother; he was having as much fun as the rest of us. We all just knew that his judgment was intact while ours wasn't.

Beau was beloved, by me most of all. He was an engaging, approachable, and striking figure, even back then. He was quick with a smile in a way that was impeccably authentic. He exuded a sense of complete confidence in who he was, whatever the situation.

People flocked to him, in any room, at every age. He was always full of energy, always needed to be doing something, whether it was playing sports or going out. He was captain of the high school tennis team and played varsity soccer. He knew early on he was headed into politics. It's what he wanted to do. He was president of his class every year.

He was also funny as hell, often with a shocking sense of humor. He could be biting, but he was never mean. He was competitive but not obsessively so—he wasn't a jackass. He was almost compulsive in the way he dressed, which later meant the same khakis or jeans, an Izod polo shirt or Brooks Brothers button-down, and a variation of the same loafers, lined up perfectly against a wall before he went to bed. He had the longest eyelashes to go with those striking blue eyes. He had great hair. He was that rare kid who other kids didn't resent for his good looks. Instead, everyone felt better just by being around him.

He didn't avoid conflict, didn't back away from it, but he was slow to create it or engage in it. We argued as kids about kid things: whose turn it was on Atari, what TV show to watch, which side of the couch the other had to stay on. Later we'd argue about the best directions to take to get somewhere and what time we needed to leave. Beau was always late, his sense of time completely warped. If we had five minutes to be somewhere, and the location was twenty-five minutes away, he'd shrug and say, "We'll make it." It drove me insane.

More than anything else, Beau was fun. He could fashion a great time out of the incredibly mundane. He loved music and he loved to drive and he usually combined the two. He was nuts about the first car that Dad got for us, a 1972 green Caprice Classic convertible with white vinyl seats, which he picked up at Manheim's Auto Auction for $2,100. He and I spent a lot of time riding in cars together, and he always had music on and he always sang along. We loved to listen to WXPN, then the free-form college radio station broadcast out of Penn. His musical tastes ran from the Grateful Dead and Crosby, Stills & Nash to early R.E.M. and the Hooters.

We were inseparable, often referred to by a single moniker: *BeauAndHunt*. We went together to every dance, every party. We double-dated, even for the prom. We had the same group of friends.

We thought alike but acted on our thoughts differently. If we went to the highest point of a cliff to jump off into a quarry's water hole, our instincts were the same: do it. But I had no filter. I'd walk up, look down, and say let's go. Beau would arrive at the same decision, but he was almost clinical. He'd inquire about the water's depth, inspect for rocks. In the end, we'd jump together. Friends viewed us as different but not as separate. Two sides of the same coin.

The biggest difference between us: I drank and Beau didn't.

CHAPTER FOUR

LOADED

The first drink I remember taking was a glass of champagne when I was eight. My dad had just been reelected to the Senate, in 1978, and I was at an election-night victory celebration at Archmere Academy in Claymont, where Dad went to high school and Beau and I would go later. I took the glass under a table and drank the whole thing. I didn't know what I was doing, really—to me, champagne was just a fizzy drink. I wasn't trying to get drunk; it would have been just as likely for me to wind up under the same table stuffing my face with a piece of cake. Someone must have looked under there at some point and spotted this eight-year-old with an empty champagne glass, acting kind of goofy. Next thing I remember, my grandfather took me outside, somewhere near the football field, to get some fresh air and straighten up.

The first drink I ever took knowing what I was doing—or, more accurately, knowing what I shouldn't be doing—was in the summer between eighth and ninth grades. I was fourteen, staying overnight at the house of my best friend, who was a year older. His parents went out for a while and we swiped a six-pack from the garage, splitting it between us. When the parents came home, we pretended to be asleep in his room because three beers at that age left us drunk off our asses. I woke up early the next morning to make nine o'clock mass and felt like shit. I got up in the middle of the service, made my way outside, and threw up. Dad thought I had the flu.

The troubling thing, looking back: Getting blasted and sick as a dog didn't scare me or turn me off one bit. Instead, I thought it was kind of cool. While I felt a nagging guilt from disappointing my father, who didn't drink and who encouraged us to stay away from alcohol as well, I wanted to do it again.

A short time later, Beau and I went away to the Finger Lakes, as we did every summer to spend several weeks with our grandparents, the Hunters—Mommy's parents, Louise and Robert. (Robert Hunter is my and Beau's son's namesake.) Their clapboard house with a wraparound porch sat on eighty wooded acres on the southern end of Lake Owasco, in the heart of God's Country, in upstate New York.

Beau and I loved our grandparents so much. They never got over their daughter's death, of course, but they embraced us, and we embraced them, in a way that helped us all continue to feel the massive amounts of love that Neilia left behind. Dad insisted that we know our mommy's parents and her life. So we spent the month of August with Mom-Mom and Da-Da at Lake Owasco, as well as every spring break at their winter home in Florida, all the way through college.

Da-Da was a restaurateur who owned a downtown diner in Auburn, New York, a classic silver dining car on the Owasco River. (You can visit Hunter's Dinerant today and see a picture of my grandparents on the wall behind the homemade pies.) As much as an eatery, it was a community gathering spot, and when my grandfather didn't see someone come in for a while, he'd visit to make sure they were all right.

The depth of his concern and generosity wasn't known to Beau and me until he died, in 1991. At his funeral, people came up to us, one after another, to say that if it hadn't been for our grandfather they never could've paid for college, or bought their first home, or started their business.

Our days up there started with making the rounds with Da-Da, all three of us packed in the front seat of his yacht-like Cadillac Eldorado. One of us rode on our grandfather's lap until we were eleven or twelve, when he'd let each of us drive by ourselves up the steep stone driveway, our heads barely peeking above the dashboard. We visited every relative within driving distance, starting with our great-grandfather and our great-aunt Winona, who didn't really speak much—she had an intellectual disability—but had the sweetest smile that lit up the world whenever we arrived.

We also spent time every trip with Mommy's two brothers: Uncle Mike, who would take us fishing, and Uncle Johnny, an electrical lineman for Niagara Mohawk who'd take us camping for a few days in his pop-up camper.

It wasn't until we were in our teens that Beau and I learned they weren't our Mommy's biological brothers. They were siblings in every way except by birth—they were actually her second cousins. Da-Da's brother, who died before I was born, was an alcoholic who had a daughter about ten years older than Mommy. She had alcohol and drug problems as well, and had two children out of wedlock. Da-Da and Mom-Mom adopted them both at birth. I don't think anyone was keeping that story from us all those years; we just always knew them as brothers who grew up together with our mommy.

Those summers were free-range bliss: mornings with Aunt Winona; learning to play lacrosse with Uncle Johnny; going to Skaneateles to see Aunt Grace and Uncle Alan, who lived next door to the house where our mommy grew up; then swimming in the lake all afternoon, or playing thirty-six holes of golf and collecting balls, often when it seemed Beau and I were the only two people on the course. Our treat afterward was Texas Hots—wieners sliced down the middle with hot sauce—and soft-serve ice cream at the Skanellus Drive-In.

We'd take day trips with Da-Da, like to the Baseball Hall of Fame in Cooperstown, two hours east. One summer the three of us found a submerged wooden boat that had washed up in the shallows of the lake. We dragged it out and spent the summer repairing and caulking it. When we finished, Da-Da rigged it with a tiny motor and off we went. Beau, Da-Da, and I were so proud of ourselves for getting it back on the lake—until the boat started taking on water as we made the turn around a second cove. We tried frantically to get it back to shore. The boat sank right where we had found it.

Those summers became so deep-rooted in our lives that Beau and I went back there together for the last time in the winter of

2014. We stayed at the lake for two days, visiting everyone we could. Six months later, Beau was dead.

But that summer before my freshman year in high school was cut short for me a couple of weeks after we arrived. The kid I drank those beers with had gone on a joyride with a girl we both knew. He was drinking as they sped down a long road, lost control of his car, and crashed into a tree. He survived, but the girl was killed—the ultimate guilt-inducing tragedy.

I returned from the Finger Lakes early to be with him. His mother had asked me to come over, believing I had the ability to be empathetic while still giving my friend his space. I stayed with him the rest of that summer. He cried every day. I just sat with him.

Yet when school started that fall, something changed. We drifted apart. I couldn't understand it at the time, but I'm sure it was because I had seen my friend all summer at his most exposed and unguarded—a horribly vulnerable place for a teenager to be. He'd shared so much pain that I think my presence was a constant reminder of it as he reentered the larger world. I'm sure he resented it as he tried to toggle between dealing with that tragedy and wanting to move on.

My freshman year was awful. I stayed at Wilmington Friends, even though Beau had gone on to Archmere, and everything felt off and awkward, including having someone I thought was a close friend turn on me. I was four feet eleven inches tall and weighed 90 pounds—I'd sprout to six feet one inch, 175 pounds less than three years later—and played on the football team. The school was small enough that almost everyone played, even if only on the varsity practice squad. I loved football—the team won state that year—but I was so undersized that I sustained concussions and broke what seemed like every bone in my body: my arm twice, my fingers, a wrist, an ankle. Older guys picked on me because I got injured so often. That hurt more than the actual injuries.

I must've been a sight. Even Beau later jokingly nicknamed me "Lucas," after the title character in the movie starring Corey Haim as a scrawny, socially inept high school freshman who wants to play football.

I was also becoming obsessed with girls, even though I hadn't hit puberty—another source of ribbing by the older players. That spring, I went with a bunch of guys to a senior party and got really wasted. All of a sudden, I felt comfortable in a crowd filled with the same kids who'd made me feel uncomfortable all year. I went up to the prettiest girl in school, a five-foot-ten-inch senior, and asked her to the prom. She basically ignored me, God bless her, and I got hazed about it later, including by my former friend.

Still, the drinking was a revelation. It seemed to solve every unanswered question about why I felt the way I felt. It took away my inhibitions, my insecurities, and often my judgment. It made me feel complete, filling a hole I didn't even realize was there—a feeling of loss and my sense of not being understood or fitting in.

I transferred to Archmere for my sophomore year. I drank in earnest in high school—mostly beer or on occasion a bottle of what-ever someone had stolen from their parents' liquor cabinet—though I didn't drink during football season, and no one drank during the school week. But there were all of these old du Pont estates in our area, so we'd have house parties inside these aging, eclectic mansions. Beau was concerned about me drinking, but he never demanded that I stop. He wasn't a scold. We never lectured each other about anything. Besides, I wasn't out of control. I wasn't driving drunk. Beau was usually driving me.

My senior year was the roughest, from beginning to end. Beau had left for Penn, and even though he was only forty minutes away, his not being home was a big change for me. The dynamics were all off.

Dad had dropped out of the Democratic primary for president a few weeks after school began. It was a confusing, angering disappointment for us all. Dad exited the campaign trail to preside as chair of the Senate Judiciary Committee over the contentious and historically consequential U.S. Supreme Court nomination of Robert Bork, one of the tensest and most consuming periods of Dad's Senate career.

All of that paled compared to Dad's life-threatening aneurysm, which knocked him down in February 1988, less than four months after Bork's nomination was rejected by the full Senate. He was rushed to Walter Reed Medical Center, where he was given last rites before surgery. My worst fear—losing Dad or Beau—seemed on the brink of coming true. He'd barely recuperated when he suffered a pulmonary embolism, and then he had surgery for another aneurysm—all within four months.

I visited him at Walter Reed almost every weekend. He was barely recognizable: tubes everywhere, head shaved, staples across his skull. Severed nerves caused the left side of his face to droop. I had no idea how things would end up—from my perspective, none of it looked hopeful—and indeed he didn't return to the Senate for seven months.

When I wasn't at Walter Reed I was mostly alone, with Beau away at school and Mom spending so much time at the hospital. I did fine in school, but honestly, I don't have many good memories from that year at all.

Then, in June, I did absolutely the last thing anybody else needed to deal with: I got busted for cocaine possession. It happened right after graduation, during Beach Week in Stone Harbor, New Jersey, an annual gathering of young knuckleheads. I'd done coke maybe three or four times before; there was a period in the spring, following football season, when guys started to use, though I wasn't one of the regulars. But on the second night of partying I was doing it with a friend and a girl from our class in a car parked outside a house party. The police came to break things up, and someone inside must have told them what we were up to. Cops knocked on our window, found the drugs, and cuffed us.

I was eighteen. I ended up doing a pretrial intervention with six months of probation, after which the arrest was expunged from my record. (I disclosed it voluntarily during a 2006 Senate committee hearing as part of my nomination to the Amtrak board of directors.)

It scared me straight—for a while. I owned up to it and didn't do coke again that summer or, really, more than a couple of times in college. Beau was surprised I did cocaine but he helped me get through it.

I knew I'd let down Dad. He was still recuperating, still in rough shape, and while he surely was upset, I also knew even then that there was nothing I could do that would stop his love. He was the strictest of any of our friends' parents—we had a curfew; if we stayed over at a friend's house we had to call him at midnight. Yet if you screwed up and it wasn't something done out of meanness or intended to be hurtful, he would love you through it. So many parents use withdrawal as punishment for their kids. That was never my dad.

This consequence was more his style: I started working twelve-hour days as a gofer at a construction site right behind our house. It was the worst job I ever had. Once, when they were building cinder-block foundations after a huge storm, I had to wade up to my waist in clay mud to mark where the blocks were. The guy operating the backhoe scooped out a huge pile of mud and water and, when I wasn't looking, dumped it right on top of me. He thought it was the funniest thing in the world.

I wanted to walk off the job right then—I should've walked off. But I knew I couldn't. That's how badly I'd screwed up in New Jersey.

Beau didn't take his first drink until he turned twenty-one, when it was legal. He drank socially after that, then quit at thirty. One reason: Dad and his vocal aversion to alcohol. Growing up, Dad had watched relatives he adored—smart, learned, working-class guys—as they engaged in these grandly intellectual conversations around his grandmother Finnegan's dinner table. Then he'd watch it all devolve into disturbing drunkenness.

Some of his relatives had struggled with alcoholism since high school. He saw it as a problem that loomed large in the family history. It scared him. He made a conscious choice not to be seduced by it and he encouraged Beau and me to do the same.

Beau could. I couldn't.

I was anxious to get to college. My first day at Georgetown I went and talked with the football coach. I ran a fast forty-yard dash and he told me to suit up—definitive proof that Georgetown football ain't

Alabama football. I played for about two weeks. It was awful. On the one hand, I was a walk-on on a team where everybody already knew each other from preseason workouts. On the other hand, because of the two-a-day practices, starting at 6 a.m., I missed out on everyone in the dorms staying up late and getting to know each other there. Not the most social person to begin with, I felt like I wasn't meeting anybody. While Beau joined a fraternity at Penn, that option did not exist for me at Georgetown. Besides, I would never put myself in a position of letting someone decide whether or not they were going to choose me. I knew what my reaction would be to someone in that situation: *Fuck you.*

I was homesick. Dad knew it. He would call with some excuse he made up about needing to remain overnight in Washington and invite to me stay with him at a hotel near the Capitol, where we'd have dinner and hang out. It was the only thing that made my first few months bearable. Though things got better, I never really settled in at Georgetown.

I drank, but usually not more than everybody else. I had a natural governor to help keep it in check: I didn't have the money to drink a lot in bars, though I did find ways around that. At the Tombs, a popular student spot, if you had enough money to buy a pitcher and knew the bartender, you could keep getting the pitcher refilled. There were times I arrived for brunch with friends and didn't leave until 2 a.m.

I spent most free weekends visiting Beau at Penn or working a part-time job parking cars for a valet company. I also became friends with several young, progressive Jesuit priests and got involved in various campus groups. These included Agape, a retreat program for spirituality; and the school's Center for Immigration Policy and Refugee Assistance, one of the country's first justice reform groups for immigrants.

Between my junior and senior years, I spent a month in Belize with the Jesuit International Volunteers—a kind of Jesuit-led blend of the Peace Corps and AmeriCorps. With a dedicated priest named Father Dziak and nine other students, we established a summer camp program for disadvantaged children in the little coastal town of Dangriga that's now taught in several other countries.

Another priest, Bill Watson, encouraged me to join the Jesuit Volunteer Corps for a year in the United States after I graduated, pointing out that there were communities in just as much need here as there were internationally. I signed up straightaway and was slotted to serve on an Indian reservation in Washington State. The four student volunteers who had been there the previous year all chose to stay, however, so I was offered a spot at a church in Portland, Oregon, instead.

I worked out of a small food bank in the church basement. I remember single mothers coming in who didn't have food for the week, or had their utilities shut off, or were being threatened with eviction. I'd advocate for them by calling the utilities to get their heat turned back on, or talk with social services to make sure their families weren't tossed out of their homes. I'd later deliver essential groceries from our food closet, mostly to seniors and mothers with small children who had no transportation. In the afternoons, I'd help with an after-school program for kids between grades three and six whose parents would then pick them up after work.

When the last kid left, I'd take a bus across town to another church that housed a socialization center for adults with intellectual disabilities, many of whom were veterans. I hung around there because of the pretty blond volunteer from Chicago who ran it: Kathleen Buhle.

We'd met during orientation. There were three Jesuit volunteer houses in Portland, each with six to eight volunteers. We'd all get together all the time. We'd pool our food allowances for potlucks and sit around and talk for hours. We came from schools all over the country—Kathleen graduated from St. Mary's in Minnesota—but we were like-minded in our idealized devotion to social justice and making the world a better place.

There was tremendous camaraderie. Our heroes were the six Jesuit priests murdered in 1989 in El Salvador. We adopted the liberation theology that they preached, radical within the Catholic Church mainstream, which emphasizes social and political concern for the poor and oppressed. We were inspired by the activist prayer: "Touch me with truth that burns like fire."

It felt freeing. Living three thousand miles from where I grew up, I almost felt like I had escaped the person everyone back there expected me to be. I was more confident, felt closer to my authentic self. I grew a beard, wore a leather jacket, rode the bus. I'd sit in Powell's Books with enough money for an endless cup of coffee, then go to Nobby's and drink nickel draft beers. I read everyone, from John Fante to Aldous Huxley to Lao-tzu. My favorite novel at the time was Charles Bukowski's *Post Office,* about a down-and-out barfly—a bleak omen, in retrospect, of where my life would one day land.

I had kept journals, written poems, and drawn in sketch pads for years, always toying with the notion of someday writing books or painting. Now I'd found an environment that seemed to nurture all of that. Dad once told me that my mother, long before she died, had said she knew even while I was in the womb that I was going to be an artist. I drew constantly as a kid, getting lost in sketching figures and concocting endless mazes on notebook paper.

Later, in my teens and throughout college, I'd share with Beau poems that I wrote and sometimes submitted anonymously to journals and magazines. He loved them and encouraged me to keep it up; he told me he wished he'd become a singer-songwriter. Dad always made it clear I could be anything I wanted to be, but I never found the courage or the confidence to take those artistic pursuits any further.

Then Kathleen got pregnant. We married four months later, on July 2, 1993. We threw an engagement party for friends and family at Dad and Mom's house in Delaware, then held the ceremony a week later in Chicago, at St. Patrick's Church, an Irish neighborhood mainstay known as Old St. Pat's because the yellow-brick building predates the Great Chicago Fire of 1871. The reception afterward was at the Knickerbocker Hotel ballroom, across the street from the Drake. Everybody had a blast. Kathleen and I were very much in love; we would've gotten married soon anyway, regardless of whether she was pregnant. Naomi, named after the sister I lost, was born that December. I was all in.

I was also at a crossroads. I had been accepted to law school at Georgetown, Duke, and Syracuse. Beau was in his second year at

Syracuse, where Dad also got his law degree, and already had his mind set on public service.

I knew Syracuse had a renowned creative writing program—one of my favorite writers, Raymond Carver, had taught there, and another favorite, Tobias Wolff, was currently on the faculty. I had applied to the MFA program and been accepted. I considered getting a joint MFA-law degree.

Now all of that sounded a little silly. Studying fiction at Syracuse was a dream that would not lend itself to supporting a family. Besides, we weren't particularly keen on living with a newborn in a place that seemed very far from home. The more grown-up choice was to go on to law school at Georgetown and shelve the artistic stuff.

That's what I did. I returned to Georgetown, though my first choice had been Yale Law, where I hadn't been accepted. Following my first year, I applied to Yale again and included with my application a poem I wrote—something everyone discouraged. Yale's acceptance letter noted that my success and dedication during my first year of law school at Georgetown more than qualified me, but that my poem was unlike anything they'd ever received and earned me my spot there.

Beau understood each step, but still was disappointed I didn't take the leap and pursue an MFA.

New Haven was a grind, scholastically and financially.

It was also a ball, in the way those periods are when you're too young and dumb to know better. I paid for tuition and room and board with loans, and bought books and food with a small Pell Grant. Kathleen and I and little Naomi lived in a tiny garden apartment we had to enter through a basement. It was so run-down that when Dad, Uncle Jimmy, Uncle Frankie, and Beau drove up to help us move in, Uncle Jimmy looked around and said, "There's no way you're living in a place like this." He enlisted the others to help tear out the thirty-year-old wall-to-wall carpeting and repaint every wall, working around the clock. As usual, Uncle Jimmy transformed a disaster into something beautiful and, in this case, turned a dilapidated rental into a quaint little home. Then we moved in our furniture, four pieces in all.

Kathleen stayed home with Naomi, a choice born as much out of necessity as of desire: we couldn't afford childcare. We took turns putting Naomi to sleep and waking up with her. We had just enough pocket change so that Kathleen could go to the movies on Tuesday nights while I stayed home with the baby, and I could go out on Thursdays, while she stayed with Naomi. I usually went to a tavern where I got to know a bartender named Flo. She knew how broke I was. If I bought two drinks, Flo gave me a third one free.

That was the entirety of our social life, except for the potlucks with people from school that we held regularly at our apartment. We were the only couple, it seemed, that had a kid.

I worked like hell. The day after the spring semester's last final exam, I started the first of two eight-week summer internships for two different law firms in Chicago. I'd return to school a week late in the fall so that I could earn that one extra paycheck. The money

I made during those sixteen weeks was what we lived on the rest of the year.

After I received my law degree in 1996, we moved back to Wilmington. I joined my father's Senate reelection bid as a deputy campaign manager, while also getting a job in the executive management training program at MBNA America, a leading credit card company that has since been acquired by Bank of America. Beau was working in Washington for the U.S. Department of Justice, and soon became a federal prosecutor in the U.S. Attorney's Office in Philadelphia.

Being a corporate lawyer was the antithesis of what I'd thought I'd be doing. But I had $160,000 in student loans from college and law school, a burgeoning family, and no savings. Whether I made money from a law firm or a bank didn't make much difference to me: I had to make money.

Much like when I turned down the chance to get an MFA at Syracuse, I felt like I had no choice. In part, it was the fear of the unknown. In my mind, I couldn't afford to work for the Justice Department or as a public defender. Obviously, people who have families and debts get by on those salaries every day. What I didn't realize until later is that whatever I made wouldn't pay enough for what Kathleen and I thought we wanted.

The first things we did were buy a house, get a decent car, and put Naomi in private school. It wasn't lavish, but we were on our way to establishing a lifestyle that's difficult to turn back from. Every decision I made after that was based on how to maintain what I had and how to make more. One private school tuition would turn into three, one car into two, the $300,000 mortgage into a $1 million mortgage. I kept climbing the escalator and didn't know how to get off.

That year after law school, we bought a big, run-down pre–Revolutionary War redo. It had been used as a boardinghouse/frat house for ten dudes between the ages of eighteen and twenty-eight. When we moved in, a refrigerator with a hole drilled through the door for the tap from a beer keg still stood in the living room. There was a pool table in the dining room. Kathleen, Beau, Dad, and I, along with a bunch of friends, went to work on restoring it—much like Dad had done with the house we grew up in. We put in new plumbing ourselves, gutted the bathroom. We tore out walls, redid floors. We scraped, caulked, primed, and repainted every square inch of the place.

Beau moved into the third floor while I covered the mortgage. Everybody we knew convened at our house. In 1998, Kathleen and I had our second daughter, Finnegan, and before long Beau started dating a dark-haired, blue-eyed woman we'd known growing up named Hallie Olivere.

We flipped the house for about twice what we paid for it. I had more money in the bank than any Biden in six generations. I helped my brother pay off his student loans. I left MBNA and got a job at the U.S. Department of Commerce as executive director for e-commerce policy. We moved to Washington and enrolled Naomi at Sidwell Friends, one of the city's most exclusive schools. The tech bubble burst not long afterward, temporarily putting a damper on e-commerce policy, so I started my own law firm/lobbying shop. I eventually worked mostly on behalf of Jesuit universities and hospitals.

Not long after our third daughter, Maisy, was born in 2000, we moved back to Delaware to be closer to family. I kept my firm in DC, started to drink more heavily after work, and missed the last train to Wilmington more and more often. I was a functional alcoholic—I always could drink five times more than anyone else—but now I was staying overnight, not making it home in time to take the kids to school in the morning.

I tried to quit drinking when we returned to Washington, in 2003. I'd stop for thirty days, then binge for three. I couldn't get control of it.

I knew what I did and did not want. I wanted to build a successful business. I wanted to get my brother elected attorney general. I wanted to run a marathon, do a triathlon. I wanted to write a book and to paint. I did not want to be an absent father. I did not want to have a partnership with Kathleen in which drinking became the fault line between us.

Later that year, with Kathleen unsure of what to do, I admitted myself into the Crossroads Centre, a residential rehab program in Antigua. Founded five years earlier by Eric Clapton, Crossroads follows a twelve-step approach modeled after Alcoholics Anonymous. I stayed there for a month. It worked.

Despite its celebrity-musician roots and Caribbean setting, Crossroads was nice but no-frills. A one-story building above the water with about twenty rooms, it offers scholarships to those who can't afford the program and admits anyone who lives on the island for free. There are no daily massages or trips to the market. There are no phones or computers. Everybody has a roommate, makes his own bed, does his own laundry, helps with chores.

I didn't know what to expect. I had a desire to be free from the compulsion to drink, but I had no idea what that meant. At age thirty-three, I couldn't imagine what I would fill my time with if I wasn't filling it with all the things connected to alcohol: drinking after work, drinking at dinner, drinking at parties, drinking while watching football games on Sundays . . .

I was immediately struck by the program's compassion, simplicity, and promise. I was incredibly moved by the hard-core, often harrowing stories told by people from all different backgrounds. They had gone through their own hells, some self-inflicted. But all told stories of trauma that gave me a new sensitivity and understanding of what people were dealing with. By the time I left, I learned how to look forward to life in a way that didn't involve needing to change the chemical equilibrium of my brain. I learned that I could fill time without a drink.

When I got home, Beau picked me up at the airport and the next day accompanied me to my first AA meeting, in Dupont Circle. It was too daunting for me to go alone.

Beau's presence proved to be serendipitous. It was an open meeting, meaning you didn't have to be an alcoholic to attend. Afterward, everyone stayed for coffee and the regulars introduced themselves to any newcomers. The goal was to find a sponsor as soon as possible—someone who had been through it all and could help you stay sober using the tools of AA's twelve steps.

If I'd gone alone, there's no doubt I would have left immediately and headed straight home. But Beau being Beau, he insisted we stay. He milled around, chatted up everybody. Before I knew it, he introduced me to Jack, who would be my sponsor for the next seven years and, for that period at least, save my life.

Politics is not the family business—service is. But politics is tied to much of that service and needs to be calculated during decisions of when to run, what to run for, and how to campaign.

One thing that was always difficult for Beau and me to game out was his political path while our dad's career continued to rise. We were as intimately involved in what Dad did politically—Senate races, presidential runs, choosing to join the Obama ticket—as we were in mapping out his own strategy.

Beau was elected Delaware attorney general in 2006, and two years later Dad's Senate seat opened up when he left for the Obama administration. The conventional wisdom was that the Democratic governor would appoint Beau to the seat until a special election was held two years later, at which time he'd be the front-runner.

Beau wouldn't have it. He wanted to be viewed as his own entity and not as someone riding in on his prominent father's coattails. The appointment went instead to Dad's friend and longtime chief of staff Ted Kaufman. There was no one more qualified to be a United States senator than Ted, who was also one of Beau's closest confidants and like an uncle to both of us. When the special election then came up, Beau had just returned from Iraq and didn't want to disrupt his family even more after being gone for a year. He set his sights on becoming governor, most likely in 2016, and neither one of us planned ahead for anything more than that.

Beau and I always knew that Dad wouldn't retire until he became president. That was the collective dream of the three of us. It was never talked about in that way, but we knew that was the trajectory.

When Dad had to decide whether to join Obama as his vice president, Beau and I privately weighed the pros and cons. My initial reaction: "You're one of the most powerful members of the Senate, you're chairman of the Foreign Relations Committee, and you can keep your own voice." Beau's reaction was less reflexive, more diagnostic, like that kid considering whether to leap into the quarry pond from the top of the cliff. "Turning down the nominee of your party in a historic election just isn't done, out of protocol," he advised. "The vice president's job will become what you make of it."

As always, Beau, Ashley, our mother, and I were the last in the room with Dad when he made his decision. Huddled at our parents' house, inside Dad's study, with its fireplace and Chesterfield couches and book-lined wall, we all agreed that Dad had both the power of persuasion and the innate loyalty needed to make that job work. We believed he would go on to become the most influential vice president ever—that is, if you discount Dick Cheney, who had the advantage of manipulating his commander in chief.

An early, up-close glimpse for us of the intensity of Dad's new position, and his ability to adapt to it, came in November 2009.

It was a fraught time, the height of an internal White House debate about whether to increase the number of U.S. troops in Afghanistan. Nevertheless, Dad kept our family's decades-old tradition of spending

Thanksgiving week in Nantucket. Beau had returned from his year of deployment in Iraq just two months earlier. The house we stayed in became, in effect, a long-distance adjunct of the West Wing, filled and surrounded by military aides and Secret Service.

Seated in armchairs inside a wood-paneled New England den, Beau and I witnessed it all, at least during those times when classified information wasn't exchanged: the stress of life-and-death stakes; political knife-fighting at the highest level; and the best traits of our dad in vivid, frenetic action.

It was a critical moment for him. One misstep could make his next three or seven years long and uncomfortable ones. The power that a vice president wields is whatever the president allows, and in that first year, the relationship between Dad and President Obama was not yet fully formed.

Dad was frustrated. He felt he was being outmaneuvered by players inside the White House, Pentagon, and State Department. He'd gambled by opposing a troop buildup, putting him largely at odds with Secretary of State Clinton, Secretary of Defense Robert Gates, and General Stanley McChrystal, who'd taken command in Afghanistan and had pressed for forty thousand additional troops.

Now he was handicapped by working from a secure phone line five hundred miles away.

He paced the room as he held an impassioned conversation with Hillary Clinton. When they finished, he put down the phone and turned to us, exasperated.

"Goddammit," he exclaimed, using us, as usual, as a sounding board to clarify his thoughts. "Axelrod's gotten in her ear!"

Beau and I downplayed his annoyance.

"What does he know, Dad?"

"He knows enough." The phone rang again: Tony Blinken, Dad's national security advisor. Dad put him on hold to take another call, from Senator John Kerry. Kerry informed Dad that McChrystal was working on Obama as they spoke.

"Goddammit!"

There would be brief lulls. Dad would explain for us everybody's argument, what their interests were, which of them were purely political and which were forward-thinking and strategic. He'd talk about the implications for the Middle East and what it meant for the continuation of NATO.

It was almost like he'd picked up where we left off around the dinner table.

Then he'd get on another line and start an extended discussion with the prime minister of France, whom he knew well. Meanwhile, faxes (yes, there were still faxes) poured in as military aides darted in and out to ensure that the lines of communication with the White House were secure. It went on like that for hours and hours.

At one point, Beau and I insisted that Dad fly back to Washington so he could be in the scrum. He didn't budge. We'd finally leave the room and take the kids into town, get everybody sandwiches. When we returned, Dad was still pacing, still on the phone, still working his case.

Obama ended up giving my dad his full ear. He eventually split the difference by temporarily calling up thirty thousand more troops and ordering a partial withdrawal within about a year. Dad had gone with his conscience and it had solidified his relationship with the president. It helped elevate his influence for the rest of that term and into the next one.

Beau and I were incredibly proud and, frankly, honored to watch the way he conducted himself while taking such a huge political risk, and also seeing how swiftly he'd adapted to his new role. It became clear to us during those five days on that little island off the coast of Massachusetts, despite Dad's initial doubts, that he had made the right call in accepting Obama's offer to be vice president.

Meanwhile, my world was upended.

By 2008, my firm was thriving. Kathleen and I had a $1.6 million house in a great Washington neighborhood and three kids at Sidwell.

I was sober.

Then Dad joined the Obama ticket and I had to find new work. Some Obama advisors vehemently opposed my lobbying and made it clear it would have to end. I scrambled to start a consulting firm, Seneca Global Advisors, named after one of the Finger Lakes near my mommy's hometown. It focused on advising small and midsized companies on opportunities to expand domestically and overseas. A year later, I agreed to advise in much the same way another private equity fund, Rosemont, run by Devon Archer, a self-made, super-motivated former college lacrosse player with a disarming charm who'd flown all over the world to raise money for his real estate investment firm, and his more risk-averse best friend from Yale, Chris Heinz, John Kerry's stepson. That company merged the two enterprises' names, Rosemont Seneca, though I continued to operate independently. A second private equity fund that Devon and Chris proposed was never started.

I was riding the escalator without an exit. I once again had huge expenses and no savings, and now I had to bust my ass to build another career from scratch. I'd take ten meetings with ten prospects to land one client—if I was lucky. That didn't seem bad until I realized I needed ten clients to cover my monthly nut—a hundred pitches. I was on the road constantly.

One thing I'd learned about staying sober over the previous seven years is that you need to be as dedicated to sobriety as you were to drinking. Through practice, perseverance, and focus—as well as service and exercise and meditation—I was able to get the same sense of well-being that alcohol once provided, as well as quiet those seemingly ever-present anxieties.

But you can't ease up.

Ever.

If you do, as I did in November of 2010, here's what happens:

You find yourself flying home from a business trip in Madrid on the red-eye. Overworked, sleep-deprived, no exercise in three months, you're grateful when a flight attendant stops by your seat and asks, as she has asked everyone around you, if you'd like a drink. Without hesitation—without really even thinking—you answer, as I answered, "I'll have a Bloody Mary."

You're off to the races.

You get home eight or nine hours later and you're greeted, as I was, by your wife and your crazy-beautiful kids. They don't know what you know: that you've been drinking. That prompts a whole new category of shame and guilt. It also prompts something more complicated: elation and relief. You have this revelation: *I just drank and I feel a hell of a lot better. The world didn't stop spinning. The plane didn't drop out of the sky. My wife didn't divorce me when I walked through the door.*

The next day, you go to work. You don't drink at all that day. Or the next. The day after that, however, if you're me, you think: *Well, a beer.* You never liked beer much anyway, so that's safe. Maybe you can at least sneak a couple of beers every once in a while because it's hard to stop thinking about those three Bloody Marys you had on the plane and how fucking good they made you feel. It's a lesser sin.

So you buy a beer, a single, on the way home from work, along with a pack of Trident. Again, the world doesn't stop; nothing horrible happens. In fact, you feel better. Later that night, you tell everybody you're going to the convenience store for a pack of cigarettes—nothing unusual if you've been, as I was, a pack-a-day smoker since college. While you're there, if you're me, you also buy a six-pack.

That lasts two days. Then you think: If I drink three of those big bottles of Chimay, an ale brewed by Trappist monks in Belgium that's 12 percent alcohol, I'll get a better buzz for about the same amount of liquid.

But that's a lot of fluid to put down and you still don't really like beer, no matter what kind of monk brews it. Why not just pick up a half-pint of vodka? A few shots would give you a lot more bang for the buck. Actually, a pint would make even more sense. And, if you're me, you take that a step further: Why not a bottle?

And there you are, drinking a bottle of Smirnoff Red every night while sitting in your garage with two coats on because it's so damn cold, watching *Game of Thrones* or *Battlestar Galactica* or whatever else you can stream on your laptop, making sure before nodding off that you stash the bottle where it won't be found.

The next day, you don't get up for work. You sleep in until nine. Everybody wants to know what's wrong. If you're like me, you act put out: "What do you mean, what's wrong? Everything's fine."

When you do show up for work, you don't go to the meeting that you're already late for. Feeling bad about that, you head to a bar.

Ad infinitum.

It only gets worse. There's now another set of stresses because you're hiding the obvious. You're not abusive; you're not stumbling around; you're not driving the kids while you've been drinking. The worst is your wife finding that empty bottle you hid in the trash. But that old sense of impending doom is back, hovering over your head like a black cloud. Everybody sees it. The people around you—family, friends, coworkers—aren't sure what to do. They're seven years removed from the last time this happened. They've almost forgotten what it's like to deal with it.

They're scared.

You're scared.

And it goes on like that until you admit to yourself you need help.

Which, finally, I did.

When I relapsed that time, Beau expressed neither shock nor dismay. He viewed it like he always viewed it: as part of the process. He assured me, "We'll work it out. Let's get back on the horse. Whatever you need me to do." He was a fierce disciple of the Biden Rule: if you have to ask for help, it's too late. He'd remind me that he was just a phone call away—and then he would call me first.

Beau was always supportive, never judgmental. He never asked what most people ask: Why? I can't overstate how helpful that was. It's an impossible question for an addict to answer. I could point to traumas, family history, genetics, the intersection of bad luck and the wrong circumstances. But I don't know the answer.

Beau understood that intuitively. He refused to believe that addiction was something I chose, believing instead that it chose me. It was something he thought he could help me fix, and he did.

My drinking couldn't have been easy for him. Only now do I realize the distance it put between us. There were all those times I was alone with it, didn't let him in. I'm sure it was confusing. But Beau handled it in his special way, always putting the onus on the alcoholism instead of on me.

After my relapse in 2010, we talked about what I should do next. I suggested returning to Crossroads. Beau thought about that for a second, said, "Okay," then booked the ticket, drove me to the airport, and walked me all the way to the security gate. When I returned, he picked me up at the airport and stayed at my house overnight.

Beau was part of every decision I made about getting sober. He was a constant, but he wasn't claustrophobic. He made my recovery almost as much a part of his daily routine as I did. He developed personal relationships with Jack and Josh and Ron and everyone I was close to in AA and stayed in regular contact with them—not to keep tabs on me but because he knew they were an important part of my life. He went to AA meetings with me while we were on vacation, just so we could spend more time together. He planned ultraphysical excursions for the two of us: adventure racing, mountain biking, kayaking, rappelling down hundred-foot-high arches in Utah. His purpose wasn't solely to have a good time. He knew I needed something to keep me motivated in my recovery.

He engrossed himself in all the things I became obsessive about. He took yoga classes with me even though he hated yoga. He asked me about books I was reading on addiction and recovery outside of the AA literature. He wanted to know how I thought the twelve steps could be applied to everyday life . . .

Wish you could've known Beau.

CHAPTER FIVE

FALLING

The first weeks after Beau's burial had the veneer of peace and purpose.

I was committed to the idea of building on my brother's legacy. I sat down with Aunt Val, Hallie, and Patty Lewis, who worked closely with Beau as a deputy attorney general, and together we started the Beau Biden Foundation for the Protection of Children. The nonprofit was an outgrowth of Beau's work fighting child abuse as attorney general and now has programs in twenty states. I continued my work on various boards and memberships, including World Food Program USA (which lobbied the government for funding for the UN's World Food Programme, winner of the Nobel Peace Prize in 2020), and the Truman National Security Project, which, among other missions, promotes veterans running for public office. I returned to my consulting business and my work with Boies Schiller Flexner, where I'd been of counsel since 2010.

Still, as the weeks passed, previously invisible fissures appeared and widened. This was especially true in my relationship with Kathleen. Some of those cracks had been there before Beau got sick, created in part by my relapses with alcohol. Without Beau, those issues were magnified. Beau was always an unflagging lodestar for me whenever a problem appeared. Now I felt at sea. Every relationship in the family was rocked to some degree by Beau's death; every relationship had to adjust.

Beau left a hole that was hard to fill.

Dad was quiet—and sad. We each dealt with our grief in ways that often were incongruent with helping each other. I made myself unavailable for affection, too easily retreating into my thoughts and fears. Dad soldiered on, as he had so many times before. He resumed the business of being vice president, which takes up an enormous amount of time and focus.

Soon after the funeral, the family planned to go away together to Kiawah Island, a white-sand retreat on the coast of South Carolina, about twenty-five miles outside of Charleston. We'd gathered there before, but this time, with the noise and emotion and ceremony of the funeral finally having subsided, we would all see how hard Beau's death was on each of us.

Then, as so often happened during my father's decades of high-profile public service, a national calamity rocked our personal agenda. A week before we were scheduled to leave for South Carolina, a twenty-one-year-old white racist opened fire with a semiautomatic pistol inside the historic Emanuel African Methodist Episcopal Church, in downtown Charleston. He murdered nine Black women and men during a Wednesday-night Bible study, reportedly telling the congregants before mowing them down, "Y'all want something to pray about? I'll give you something to pray about." Victims included the church's forty-one-year-old pastor and state senator, Clementa Pinckney.

Our family arrived at Kiawah the following Tuesday. Dad attended the memorial service three days later, where, from behind a purple-draped pulpit, President Obama brought together the congregation, the victims' families, and the rest of the country with his tearful rendition of "Amazing Grace."

I went with Dad two days after that to Emanuel's regular Sunday service. We never really discussed going. One of us just asked, "What do you think we should do?" and we both immediately thought, "Of course we should go." Dad had arranged to attend quietly and without notice. He hoped that his appearance, so soon after his oldest son's death, would be a source of strength for a congregation in such pain and that they, in turn, would be a source of strength and grace for him.

We drove into Charleston early that morning. The church was packed. I love going to AME churches. It's such a welcoming community, and I always find it to be an uplifting experience. Beau and I had attended countless services with Dad since we were kids, in Delaware and elsewhere across the country.

Dad seemed to know everyone. He had spent a lot of time in South Carolina over the decades and had deep roots in the Black community. Early in his career, he campaigned for a dying breed of white Southern Democrat, like the state's longtime junior senator Fritz Hollings, as these politicians reversed their positions on civil rights. With alternatives like Strom Thurmond, they served as a transition until a generation of Black leadership, energized by the civil rights movement my Dad saw up close in Wilmington, began to rise. Dad's friendship with James Clyburn, the highest-ranking African American in Congress, dates back to the early 1980s, and in speaking about his late wife Emily, the congressman has said that "there's nobody Emily loved as a leader in this country more than she loved Joe Biden, and we talked about Joe all the time."

Dad hadn't planned to speak publicly to the congregation, filled that Sunday with visitors from all over the country. But Reverend Norvel Goff Sr., the pastor who had replaced the murdered Reverend Pinckney, spoke directly to us from the pulpit—about loss and grief and understanding—and then asked Dad to take the pulpit and say a few words.

"I wish I could say something that would ease the pains of the families and of the church," Dad began, the familiar trace of hurt and empathy in his tone. The crowded church was hushed and rapt. "But I know from experience, and I was reminded of it again twenty-nine days ago, that no words can mend a broken heart. No music can fill a gaping void . . . And sometimes, as all preachers in here know, sometimes even faith leaves you just for a second. Sometimes you doubt . . . There's a famous expression that says faith sees best in the dark, and for the nine families, this is a very dark, dark time."

The congregation stood as one for Dad after he read a verse from Psalms ("People take refuge in the shadow of your wings") and stepped down from behind the pulpit.

Afterward, Joe Riley, Charleston's longtime mayor, grabbed us and led us down to Reverend Pinckney's tiny basement office underneath the two-hundred-year-old brick church. On one wall was a photo of Reverend Pinckney with Dad, taken just months before. Both of us were moved to tears, though the truth is we had both been crying throughout the service.

Being inside Emanuel that day was an emotional, uplifting, beautiful thing. The outpouring of love and shared grief that Dad and I received and returned was indeed a source of strength. There was an enormous amount of cross-commiseration: it seemed as if every single parishioner came up and gave us both a big hug and a kiss and a cry. As was true of those who came up to us during the week between Beau's death and his funeral, listening to others' heart-breaking stories only underscored that loss is not unique.

There were moments when I felt guilty for being extended so much sympathy, especially when I knew so many of the people extending it had experienced tragedies far worse than mine. It staggered me to think about how so many of them had faced their losses without the love and resources available to me.

There were also times, I have to admit, when I felt as if no one else could understand my pain. It seemed narcissistic even to contemplate. Yet that didn't make it feel any less true. Believing that your pain is exceptional doesn't lessen anyone else's.

Pain is our universal condition. People can go through life without finding love, but no one lives for long without experiencing real hurt. It can connect us or it can isolate us. I vacillated between the two.

Those were thoughts that overwhelmed me on that sad, triumphant day in Charleston, then the epicenter of America's pain.

*   *   *

I continued to experience bouts of hopefulness and hopelessness. My dad and I struggled, neither of us knowing quite how to put our finger on what we wanted to say. When I looked into his eyes I saw what struck me as insurmountable sadness—as well as concern for me. It wasn't just that Beau was missing. The question that lingered was bigger than that, and one we hadn't yet answered for ourselves: If we weren't the three of us anymore, what were we?

At one point, I remember telling Dad, "I don't know if I should be grateful or angry at you for making us all love each other so much."

He took it the way it sounded, which was as a pretty spectacular compliment. And it was, in one way. Yet I also meant it in a more literal sense. I just felt so much pain, as I know he did and still does.

I tried to keep my focus on my kids and family and the things that gave me a real sense of meaning and motive.

I then allowed one moment, and all the underlying anger and confusion it unleashed, to give me the excuse to drink again. It was an almost instantaneous reaction, at once impulsive and short-sighted and, perhaps, inevitable.

Virtually everything I did afterward, for the next four years, resulted in me stumbling, then sliding, then racing downhill.

On July 2, Kathleen and I took our traditional anniversary walk: one mile for each year we'd been married. The twenty-two-mile trip that warm, overcast day started in Georgetown, looped past the

Washington Monument and Lincoln Memorial, then crossed the Potomac River and followed a rolling towpath nearly to Mount Vernon. We then retraced our steps back home.

Along the way, we discussed our marriage: past, present, and future. There was plenty to talk about. We were on rocky ground. If you're married to someone for twenty-two years, there are twenty-two million reasons to get a divorce. To my mind, however, there are not many good ones.

Kathleen had said, "Tell me everything; let's get everything out in the open that we can." I owned up to all my shortcomings—every grievance, every secret, every sin. We talked about our lack of intimacy, my being consumed by work and keeping up with our crushing bills, my past bouts with drinking, and how I was addressing those problems now. I hadn't had a drink in months. Some things were more troublesome than others, but I didn't think any of them rose to the level of ending our marriage. I was committed—recommitted—to making it work.

The next day we met with a couples' counselor whom we had worked with together for a while and who more recently I'd been seeing alone. She was aware of our anniversary tradition and asked how it went. I responded enthusiastically. I said it had been cathartic and felt that we'd come to a better understanding of where we stood. I said it left me feeling hopeful.

Then Kathleen answered. It was as if we had walked twenty-two miles in opposite directions. Her take, basically: "Cathartic? Who are you kidding? You can say that you're sorry for the rest of your life and it wouldn't matter. I'm never going to forgive you."

I was floored. In that moment, everything we'd said to each other the day before seemed for naught—seemed like utter bullshit. It felt like Kathleen had made the decision that we were over on the day Beau died and that the conversation we'd had driving home after his funeral really had been the end.

I snapped. I did the kind of counterproductive thing that every good alcoholic knows how to do in times of deep frustration: I set out to prove her right.

I walked out of the session, bought a bottle of vodka, and drained it.

Within weeks I was back in rehab.

I didn't want to burden my dad with the problems of my marriage, with my doubts and loneliness. I only wanted to project to him a sense of well-being. Not only was he dealing with Beau's loss while continuing to perform the duties of his office, but he was also in the midst of deciding whether to run for president in 2016.

The only recourse to salvaging my marriage and returning home was to enroll in another rehab program and stay 100 percent sober. Kathleen made that clear: I wasn't permitted back into the house until I met those criteria. I didn't think it was the best thing for me, my problem, or my kids, but I didn't think she knew what else to do.

I became an outpatient for about a month at a facility at the University of Pennsylvania, living during that period in my uncle Jimmy's house in Philadelphia. Therapists prescribed two drugs for me, one to lessen my cravings, another to make me feel sick to my stomach if I drank. I didn't test the effect of the latter. The effect of the first drug was middling.

I spent the following month at an inpatient program on a rural mountaintop about seventy miles west of Philly. I enrolled there under an assumed name, Hunter Smith, which in itself made it difficult to share the realities of what I was going through. There were times during group sessions when it almost felt like I was playacting—performing a facsimile of my story rather than confessing it. The greatest value to being in rehab is the opportunity to be honest with yourself and the other patients there, most if not all of whom are strangers. Yet for me to talk as "Hunter Smith" about the loss of someone as close to me as my brother felt less than authentic, particularly when so many had seen me give his eulogy on TV less than two months before.

I'm convinced that depriving someone for a month or more at a time of the most important relationships in his or her life—in my case, my three daughters—is too often a critical failure in how addicts are treated. I felt only one thing there: alone. Yet to have any chance of returning home, it's what I had to do.

That fall, I moved into an apartment in Washington, a second-story two-bedroom in a new building on the corner of Eleventh Street and Rhode Island Avenue, near Logan Circle. It was across the street from a skate park and catty-corner to a liquor store. It was the first time in forty-six years that I lived by myself. Instead of going home every night to be embraced by three children I adored, I returned to a strange, silent space. I slept only on the couch; the idea of sleeping in a bed by myself heightened my gnawing sense that Kathleen already knew she was never letting me come back.

I went to therapy three days a week and met with a sober coach. I toted around a portable Breathalyzer with a built-in camera, blowing into it four times a day as it fed a live image to a remote counselor, making sure I didn't sneak a drink. I attended yoga sessions six times a week, and at my therapist's urging went two nights a week to a self-realization program in Aberdeen, Maryland, a ninety-minute drive each way. Throughout all that, I maintained my consulting business, downsized as it was.

I still went to my daughters' soccer games and other extracurricular activities outside the house, and Naomi was now attending Penn. I was also able to spend more time with Beau's kids, Natalie and Hunter. A shared-travails bond began to form between Hallie and me. She became someone to confide in—at that point, nothing more. My anger, some justified, some not, served for me as its own counterintuitive motivation: I was going to get sober and get better, dammit, but no longer beg Kathleen to be her husband.

That October, my dad announced he would not run for president in 2016. He talked publicly about the impact of Beau's death on him and our family, and the need for more time to recover. He didn't talk about the other dynamic in the equation: the prevailing attitude among Democratic Party influencers that it was Hillary Clinton's turn, a dividend she'd earned from her narrow primary loss to Obama and her service afterward as secretary of state. For Dad to compete, it would have been an uphill climb from the start.

I don't know if my relapses figured into his calculation. They certainly couldn't have helped, but that's not something Dad would ever say. I encouraged him to run. My dad saw how hard, if choppily, I was working to get sober. More than anybody, he knows this one thing: adversity brings our family closer together.

By then, the fall air had turned cooler and the light angled lower. All the old daily rhythms that revolved around Beau seemed off. I no longer called him, or answered his call, three times a day, like clockwork, arguing almost as much as we laughed. I no longer walked into my parents' house to find him already there, half joking about the expired jar of mayonnaise in the back of the refrigerator.

Everything I drove past, it seemed, triggered his memory: the Amtrak station where we basically were raised; the railroad tracks we hiked up and down as kids; the Charcoal Pit, where we ordered triple-thick black-and-white milkshakes, cheesesteaks, and well-done fries. Even seeing a duck fly by—Beau loved those damn ducks.

This strange new normal quickened during the holidays. My girls were traumatized by Beau's death and confused by their family seeming to disintegrate before their eyes. I kept telling them, "Your mom and I, we'll figure this out. Don't be mad. It's not your mom's fault. It all revolves around my drinking or not drinking." But that was bullshit. It felt as if everyone was waiting for me to lose it and prove their point.

Which I did, beginning the week before Christmas.

Each year on December 18, our immediate family, along with a handful of longtime friends, gather for the anniversary of my mommy's and baby sister's deaths. We'd meet in Wilmington for 7 a.m. mass at St. Joe's, then head to my parents' house for coffee and Danish or bagels. Dad and Beau and I would visit the grave sites to lay a wreath topped with three white roses. Now, Beau rested fifteen feet away.

In past years, Kathleen and I would come up the night before with the girls, who were out of school by then, so we could all go to the service in the morning. We'd then stay in Delaware through Christmas morning, when we'd all fly to Chicago to be with Kathleen's family at their lake house.

This anniversary, however, Kathleen called to tell me the girls weren't coming to Delaware until Christmas Eve, and that she didn't want me accompanying them to Michigan City for Christmas.

I was shattered. I see now that what she was trying to do was to protect our girls. As much as it hurt me, I was the threat that she needed to protect them from. It's a hard-earned wisdom—as an addict, you often force the ones closest to you to make the tough decisions, things that can break a relationship beyond repair. But those same actions can save the innocents around you from a far greater pain. Kathleen was brave in these moments, and I've only come to appreciate that now.

I wasn't thinking about any of that back then. Hours after Kathleen's call, I started drinking secretly, though I backed off enough to prevent it from becoming a full-blown binge. My daughter Naomi's birthday is on December 21, another day we usually spent at my parents', and I couldn't see her then, either; I'd already missed Finnegan's and Maisy's birthdays in August and September because I was in rehab.

Christmas followed in no time. The girls left with Kathleen. Mom and Dad flew to the Caribbean with Uncle Jimmy and Aunt Val, like they did every Christmas. Hallie and her kids headed to Florida with another family.

Beau was dead.

Alone, depressed, angry, my brain humming with an alcoholic's illogic, I bought a bottle of vodka, retreated into my DC apartment, and drank. I did that practically every day, all day, from Christmas until the end of January.

I would turn on the TV, sit on the couch, drink, pass out. Even drunk—especially drunk—I never slept in my bed. I'd watch the TV nearly comatose, staring at it without really being aware of what was on. Other times, I'd cry for hours without realizing I was crying. I hardly ate.

I phoned it in at work, with the five employees in my office taking up the slack. I sat in on some conference calls, canceled meetings, didn't go to the office. I scratched all business trips. The only calls I took were from my daughters and my dad, who called incessantly. He'd ask how I was. I'd say fine, hang up, pass out, wake up, drink more.

I would drink like that for twelve to sixteen hours. When I finished a bottle, I'd trek across the street to Logan Circle Liquor, a sagging storefront filled with racks of booze and a clerk who worked behind a bulletproof plastic window. I'd order a handle of Smirnoff vodka—about a half gallon—in a tremulous voice and pay for it with shaky hands. Usually I'd head straight home, but sometimes the block-long trip proved to be too much: somewhere between crossing the street and climbing the stairs to my apartment, I'd unscrew the cap and sneak a swig.

I wouldn't realize that whole days, even weeks, had passed. Each one bled into the next, while simultaneously crawling by at a glacial pace. Before long I began to wake up with debilitating withdrawal symptoms. It became a chore just to raise my head off the pillow. If there wasn't a last swig left in the bottle, it took a Herculean effort to put on my boots and jacket and stumble back to the liquor store. The short walk soon felt like a marathon; then, like I was crawling over broken glass.

I had never drunk like that before. I'd drunk to excess, to the point where I knew it was no longer smart to keep drinking—that's how it was when I decided to get sober in 2003 and again in 2010. But I'd never been in such pain that I couldn't go out, that I almost couldn't go on. I lost twenty pounds. I didn't eat anything much beyond what was available at the liquor store: Doritos, pork rinds, ramen noodles. Eventually my stomach couldn't even handle the noodles.

I was drowning myself in alcohol.

I pulled out of the free fall just once. Three weeks in, unshaven and shedding weight, I saw on my calendar a commitment I'd made months earlier that I couldn't back out of: a weeklong trip to the Middle East with a U.S. delegation for World Food Program USA.

It was too important; lives literally depended on it. So, as I'd done plenty of times before, I pulled out the drunk's hole card and did what to others might seem impossible: transformed myself into a functional alcoholic. I showered, shaved, packed, and boarded a plane for Beirut.

Our first visit was to a refugee camp in Lebanon, next to the Syrian border. On the other side, 700 men, women, and children were stranded in a windswept no-man's-land with barely any assistance. They were pleading to join the 80,000 other Syrians housed in Jordan's Zaatari refugee camp, a teeming but well-organized shelter that we also would soon visit, talking with families housed in metal shipping crates that dotted a treeless, unpaved stretch of sand. Following those sojourns, I would head to Amman to lobby King Abdullah II, one-on-one, for their entry.

I'd been dropped into desperate spots around the world for the WFP many times before. Each left an indelible mark.

For instance, in December of 2013, I flew to the Philippines a month after it was lashed by Typhoon Haiyan, whose winds as high as 190 miles per hour wiped out whole swaths of the country. More than 6,000 people were killed and 4.1 million displaced. At the time, it was the largest typhoon in recorded history.

When we landed on the southernmost tip of Samar Island, in Guiuan, it looked as if someone had taken an industrial-sized scythe and cut every tree in half for as far as the eye could see. What Haiyan didn't demolish, storm surge washed away. The town's mayor, standing in an office with no walls and no roof, called the typhoon *delubyo*—Armageddon.

Yet those who survived were nothing short of astonishing. Throngs of kids swarmed us, so many of them smiling. A two-year-old clambered into my arms and wouldn't let go, clinging to me as I toured the devastation. Everyone told survival stories: clutching a tree, hiding under a hut, carrying neighbors on their shoulders through rising floodwaters.

The WFP had mobilized pre-positioned food supplies within hours of the typhoon's landfall—rice from Sri Lanka, high-energy biscuits from Bangladesh—and everyone we met was appreciative and energetic and incredibly generous with one another. Amid all that loss, it turned out to be one of the most inspiring trips I'd taken to a place where people had just experienced their darkest moment. Their hope and perseverance were infectious.

More common was the kind of heartbreak prevalent during a visit in 2011 to the Dadaab refugee camp in Kenya, near Somalia. More than 200,000 refugees and asylum seekers had fled drought, famine, and conflict to settle at a complex set in the middle of a semi-arid outback. It is the third-largest such encampment in the world.

Starvation and malnutrition were inescapable. Mothers told me harrowing accounts of crossing the Somali desert with five children and arriving in Dadaab with only two—the others were killed by lions. Established in 1991 in response to what relief workers hoped would be a temporary crisis, the camp now spanned generations.

The stark realization of what it's like to exist as a stateless person—with nowhere to return to, no community to live in beyond the camp's perimeter, being dependent on governments with no direct interest in your fate or freedom—was disturbing on an almost fathomless level.

My trip to the Middle East had its own challenges. I landed there battling my grief, my alcoholism, and my knowledge that I was advocating for people whose stakes were, at base, life-and-death.

Accompanied by Rick Leach, CEO of World Food Program USA, and fellow board member and former Secretary of Agriculture Dan Glickman, I arrived at the royal palace in Amman at the end of our six-day mission.

We had come from Beirut, where we'd spent most of each day driving through tense neighborhoods to meet with the prime minister, a UN-appointed administrator, and other players and actors with that chaotic government feeling the enormous economic and social pressure caused by the influx of a million-plus Syrians. We discussed the WFP's push for more assistance through an electronic debit card system that would benefit both refugees and the deteriorating local economy. There were a lot of moving parts and competing agendas; discussions were arduous. We would eventually get enough cash aid to launch the program in Lebanon without violence or incidents in the many pop-up camps throughout the country.

Now our goal was to convince King Abdullah II to allow more Syrian refugees into Jordan's Zaatari camp. The king was understandably reluctant: he feared infiltration by ISIS or other terrorists.

We arrived at the royal palace and were escorted to the king's office door. I entered alone. The only reason the king had agreed to meet, after many denied requests from WFP headquarters in Rome, was out of respect for my dad. I guess you could chalk it up to nepotism, in the best possible way.

I sat down across from the bright, personable king, a descendant of the Prophet Muhammad, with thoughts of my hotel room's minibar intermittently racing through my head. I was determined during the trip to regulate my drinking. I kept it private inside my room, walking the tightrope between being debilitated by the DTs because I didn't drink enough, and drinking too much to be effective. Now, I was sweating beneath my shirt but not through my jacket.

The king spoke first about our families and how much he respected my father. He went on about how my dad not only speaks with knowledge and experience but always tells the truth—which, in the king's estimation, was the foremost compliment he could pay someone engaged in the high-stakes politics of war and peace. He appreciated how blunt my dad was while still managing to remain diplomatic. They were cut from similar cloth: steeped in history, respectful, relaxed.

I'd come to advocate for refugees but also to listen and learn. We exchanged thoughts on the historical context affecting the dynamics throughout the region. The king made it clear that he was working from a place between empathy and realism. He saw the situation as a life-or-death struggle both for the refugees and for Jordan, expressing to me the tenuousness of national security in a region as volatile as his. One mistake could cost lives. Yet he was vetting refugees wanting entry into Zaatari even as we spoke.

I was fully engaged: thoughts of those vodka mini-bottles back at my hotel were quickly subsumed by the gravity of our conversation. Lives were on the line. The discussion went on for nearly an hour, just the two of us.

When we finished, King Abdullah spoke briefly with Rick, who then took the lead as we met in another part of the palace with one of the king's aides and had a more detailed discussion about programs the WFP hoped to implement in Zaatari.

Not long after we returned to the States, King Abdullah let many of the isolated refugees in Syria into Zaatari. My meeting was not the only determining factor in persuading him; there were many others advocating for these desperate, proud people. But it clearly helped. More important, considering my personal battles at the time, I hadn't blown it. I hadn't cost innocent lives.

That accomplished, I needed to get back to my apartment, uncap a bottle, lock the door.

I picked up where I left off—with a vengeance. I soon was drinking to avoid the physical pain caused by not drinking. Forget the underlying roots of alcoholism—unresolved trauma, genetics, disease—I was drinking now just to banish the ache of withdrawal. I felt lucky if I passed out. I'd be in such physical pain if I went any length of time without a drink that every joint in my body felt like it had been soldered shut. My anxiety spiked so high I'd wake with the pillow soaking wet and the couch cushions drenched with sweat, as if someone had poured a bucket of water over me. I'd have chills and a fever until I threw down another drink. Then, for an instant, it would all go away. But that effect became harder and harder to achieve. If a shot of vodka gave me relief at the start, I soon required a tumbler, then a full Collins glass, then a full fifth, just to maintain some kind of equilibrium.

Eventually it became too much for me to even pour a drink. I'd use a kitchen knife to remove the plastic nub that controls the pour on a handle of vodka, then drink straight from the bottle. Given my weakened state, even that required some finesse: I learned to twist and contort my body in such a way as to lessen the weight of the bottle, to make it more manageable. I must have looked like a cartoon moonshiner throwing back gulps from a jug.

Alcohol is a harrowing drug to be terrorized by. You really do need to keep drinking to stay alive, not just to get drunk, at least if you're drinking at the preposterous level I was. The only way to stop safely is to clinically detox, meaning to do it while in the hands of professionals. Otherwise, it was clear to me, you could die.

I stopped answering the phone altogether, not picking up for my dad, for my daughters, for anybody. My yoga instructor called once from outside my front door. I let it go. While I put work on pause, not pursuing new business, I paid bills with the legacy pieces of contracts I still had, with clients like HNTB, a global infrastructure design company, and several private equity firms. By then I was also receiving a substantial monthly fee from Burisma, the energy company in Ukraine whose board I'd joined in early 2014.

The last thing I wanted was Dad showing up in front of my apartment building with his massive security detail. But almost a month in, he'd had enough. He reduced his security to a minimum and knocked on my door. I let him in. He looked aghast at what he saw. He asked if I was okay and I told him, sure, I was fine.

"I know you're not fine, Hunter," he said, studying me, scanning the apartment. "You need help."

I looked into my dad's eyes and saw an expression of despair, an expression of fear, even—fear that I wasn't going to be able to save myself. I knew he wouldn't leave until I agreed to do something—that at this point he'd take control physically in some way if he had to. I wanted to avoid that at all costs. I was in no shape to have an emotional discussion about Beau or my pain or his pain or the utter depression and hopelessness I felt. I knew he was right—I was anything but fucking okay. I was locked in an unrelenting drinking binge that was not in any way sustainable.

I finally told him I knew of a program out west where I could get sober and heal. He made me promise to follow through, said that he'd be back to make sure. He hugged me tight, and I walked him to the door.

There was no drama, no fireworks. Two days later, I flew to the Esalen Institute retreat center in Big Sur, California, where I'd previously gone through a twelve-step yoga retreat that had helped me for a while. This time I essentially detoxed myself while I was around others participating in various programs. I got better and left there to ski alone for a week at Lake Tahoe, retracing the same runs Beau, Dad, and I covered years ago. I returned home clean, healthy—and alive.

Dad saved me. When he knocked on my door, he jolted me out of whatever state I was in and saved me by making me want to save myself. Left on my own, I'm certain I would not have survived.

That was Dad. He never let me forget that all was not lost. He never abandoned me, never shunned me, never judged me, no matter how bad things got—and, believe me, from here on they would get much, much worse. There's a popular theory that an addict needs to hit bottom before he or she can be helped. The addicts I know who hit bottom are dead. So as busy as Dad always was, he never, ever gave up on me.

I believe it's because Dad needed me. And by me, I don't mean *me*. In many ways, the greatest expression of his love was the love he had for me and Beau. I was now what remained of that. This isn't to say he doesn't love my sister just as much or love my mother most of all. But Beau and I always believed that Dad truly thought, as we both did, there was something singular the three of us shared. As a consequence, he never allowed me to fade away, never let me escape, no matter how often during the next three and a half years I tried. There were times when his persistence infuriated me—I'd attempt to fade to black through alcoholism or drug addiction, and then there he was, barging in again with his lantern, shining a light, disrupting my plans to disappear.

Disappearing was the most profound betrayal of the love that existed between us. It's what I tried instead of suicide.

CHAPTER SIX

BURISMA

The episode that led to the impeachment of a president and landed me in the heart of the decade's biggest political fable is most remarkable for its epic banality.

It contains no clandestine, cloak-and-dagger, international hocus-pocus. There's no criminal sexiness, no corrupt moral bottom to make other bad actors feel better about themselves.

There is, in short, no there here—except in the up-is-down, self-dealing universe cooked up for political and personal gain by Trump and Giuliani and their circle of bandits.

My five-year involvement on the board of Burisma Holdings, one of the largest private natural gas producers in Ukraine, ultimately has its roots, as does so much else in my life at the time, in the circumstances surrounding my brother's grave illness.

I want to be clear: Beau's health problems didn't prompt me to do something I wouldn't have done otherwise. The money was helpful, but I could've figured out another way to make it. I wasn't desperate. Yet it did provide me the ability not to work as hard at continuing to develop clients, the most time-consuming part of my work—drilling twenty dry wells to finally hit pay dirt. That gave me more time to tend to Beau.

I'd learned of Beau's tumor just months before I received a call regarding Burisma from Devon Archer, one of my business colleagues from Rosemont Seneca. Our deal with the biggest potential was a partnership with a Chinese private equity fund seeking to invest Chinese capital in companies outside the country. I was an unpaid advisor in that deal, and to this day have collected no money from the transaction. Yet, like everything else, it has joined the ever-swelling club of Trump's conspiratorial delusions, from birtherism to QAnon.

In 2013, Dad asked my then-teenage daughter Finnegan to join him on *Air Force Two* to Japan and then on to Beijing, where he was meeting with President Xi Jinping. Dad often asked his grandkids to accompany him on overseas trips. It was his chance to catch up. I jumped on the plane from Japan to China to spend time with them both. While we were in Beijing, Dad met one of Devon's Chinese partners, Jonathan Li, in the lobby of the American delegation's hotel, just long enough to say hello and shake hands. I was meeting with Li as a courtesy call while I was in the country; the business deal had been signed more than a week earlier. Li and I then headed off for a cup of coffee.

And that was that—until Trump declared I walked out of China with $1.5 billion. It's a figure that was plucked from a statement made by a company official at the time who said that was the amount the firm hoped eventually to raise. The actual amount raised before that trip to China: $4.2 million. I had no equity in the company at the time and only bought a 10 percent stake after my father left office.

A couple of months later, Devon was traveling to raise money, domestically and internationally, for his real estate investment fund, a venture I was not a part of. During one such trip to Kyiv, he met Mykola Zlochevsky, the owner and president of Burisma.

The encounter came at a critical moment for modern Ukraine. After President Viktor Yanukovych rejected an EU trade deal in 2013, Ukrainians flooded the main square in the capital city of Kyiv, demanding economic and human rights reforms and an end to the regime's massively corrupt, Putin-backed kleptocracy. Protests continued for three months, into the brutally cold winter. Government security forces finally stormed the protesters' encampments and shot into crowds, killing dozens and leaving bodies to bleed out in the streets. Ukrainians burned tires and barricaded themselves against a larger massacre that felt inevitable. It was a full-blown revolution.

Yanukovych fled for the border under the cover of night and turned up in Moscow, where he's now in exile and wanted in Ukraine for high treason. But there was no time for celebration in Kyiv. A nation still reeling from so much bloodshed and mayhem at the hands of its government now witnessed a brazen military operation carried out by inscrutable "little green men"—masked Russian special forces in unmarked uniforms. They took over military and government sites across Crimea, the Black Sea peninsula soon annexed by Putin. Russian troops then massed along Ukraine's eastern border, near where many of Burisma's natural gas fields are located—fields Russia coveted. Zlochevsky and other Ukrainians viewed Putin as a creeping threat to the country and, by extension, to Burisma.

After returning from Kyiv, Devon told me about his talk with Zlochevsky, Ukraine's former minister of ecology and natural resources, who cofounded Burisma in 2002. Smart, serious, imposing—six feet two inches tall and at least 250 pounds, with a shaved head, booming laugh, and essentially no neck—Zlochevsky was concerned with protecting his company from Putin's advances.

Toward that end, Zlochevsky wanted to lure more U.S. and European investors, both as a way to grow his business and as a show of solidarity with the West. He saw that solidarity as a bulwark against Russia's aggression. To enhance those ties, he wanted to ensure that Burisma's business practices adhered to Western standards of corporate governance and transparency.

That's a big ask in Ukraine, long in the lower tier of most-corrupt-country rankings.

To help burnish Burisma's reputation, Zlochevsky was putting together a board of directors that included non-Ukrainians with name recognition and global contacts. His most prominent get was Aleksander Kwasniewski, former president of Poland and a pro-democracy stalwart.

Devon said he had raised my name for a possible board seat—along with his own. Kwasniewski soon reached out to me. He rolled out his firsthand assessment of the threat Russia posed to an immature democracy like Ukraine. He framed Burisma as critical to maintaining the country's independence.

A compelling orator, Kwasniewski delivered a pitch to me that was impassioned, even poetic. He underscored the importance of the historical moment. The Soviet Union's chokehold on the region was still recent history for him: Poland and Ukraine were under Soviet control just over two decades earlier. He said the notion that the Iron Curtain couldn't descend again overnight was a Western fantasy.

"Russia without Ukraine is just Russia," he explained. "Russia with Ukraine is the Soviet Union."

He then brought up the recent elections of right-wing populists in Poland, as well as the sprouting of pro-Russia demagogues in once-budding democracies throughout Eastern Europe.

Russia's push into Ukraine was Putin's attempt to annex not only land and people, he said, but also the most profound sectors of the country's economy, with energy being chief among them.

"The only bulwark against that aggression," Kwasniewski pronounced near the end of his call with me, "is to strengthen the independent, nongovernmental entities that can give Ukraine the chance to blossom."

It was inspiring. It was consequential.

And, to be honest, the pay was good.

There's no question that the board fee, five figures a month, appealed to me. It wasn't out of line with compensation given to board members at some Fortune 500 companies, but I wasn't used to such a handsome sum for that kind of work. My position on the board of World Food Program USA was voluntary, and Amtrak had only paid my expenses.

Yet the fee came at an especially fortuitous juncture. I was spending so much time with Beau and his urgent medical needs that my business was being neglected. I'm not saying I would not have taken Burisma's offer if Beau hadn't gotten sick—the money helped.

"This is private industry—of course you're getting paid," Kwasniewski said to me at one point, addressing whatever dissonance I might have felt between idealism and generous compensation.

He added, "You can get paid by the Russians or the people who are fighting them."

I was interested but cautious.

I did my due diligence. When dealing with international businesses, the line between the good guys and bad guys can get murky. Most companies outside the U.S. operate in a gray area when it comes to markets and the rules they have to abide by. U.S. companies adhere to the Foreign Corrupt Practices Act, which applies U.S. law to any American corporate entity in its domestic and international operations. It's why a company like, say, ExxonMobil can't simply bribe the president of Papua New Guinea for drilling rights. Enforcement for companies elsewhere is less stringent.

I brought Burisma to Boies Schiller Flexner, the New York–based law firm where I was of counsel. With offices around the country and in London, Boies Schiller is as savvy internationally as any firm in the world, and they wanted to see whether Burisma was legit or plagued with corruption before taking them on.

Burisma showed me a report done by Kroll, a leading corporate investigations firm and publisher of a widely read annual assessment called the *Global Fraud and Risk Report*. While the report gave the company a clean bill of financial health, it was a year and a half old. That concerned me.

Boies Schiller then hired Nardello & Co., another global investigator. Founded by a former federal prosecutor, Nardello specializes in looking into foreign companies for bribery and other corrupt practices. They poked into Burisma's operations to make sure its assets were legitimately held and that the international community viewed it as a trustworthy enterprise. That's how it would win the support of allies and wary investors, and how it would continue to expand.

Burisma checked all the important boxes. There were questions about the propriety of awarding contracts to a company Zlochevsky owned while he was Ukraine's ecology and natural resources minister. That's the kind of situation where things can get gray. But the reality is that there weren't many viable privately owned natural gas companies in Ukraine, like Burisma, at the time. The vast majority of production was state owned, but Burisma also had a much higher efficiency rate than the state.

(I should note that none of the investigators knew of a probe into Zlochevsky that had just gotten under way in the United Kingdom. Officials there froze Zlochevsky's London bank accounts containing $23 million while they looked into money-laundering allegations. The UK's Serious Fraud Office eventually unfroze the assets in early 2015 and dropped the case three years later.)

Like many others outside the region, I still didn't fully comprehend how far and deep the tentacles of Russian corruption had reached in Ukraine. It astounds me to this day how involved Russia is in everything. It's hard to disassociate anyone in the region who has had success in any way with the innately dirty hands of Russia.

In my investigation before joining the board, I looked at whether or not Zlochevsky was a known criminal. I looked at whether or not he operated a business that was transparent and coherently linked to Western norms of corporate governance. I did not drill down to determine whether or not Zlochevsky acquired his wealth fairly during the decades of kleptocracy and corruption that dated back to when Ukraine was a former republic of the Soviet Union.

In Zlochevsky, I saw someone who was attempting to break with Russian influence, whether out of self-interest or some form of patriotism. I know it was driven by much more than self-preservation. He was looking to the West at a critical time, when there was a need for this company, in particular, to exist independently and out of reach of Putin and the clutches of the Russian kleptocracy.

Putin wants Ukraine for four very well-defined reasons: he wants natural resources, specifically natural gas; he wants the port in Crimea; he wants a land bridge between the Far East and Europe; and he wants a buffer between Russia and NATO to increase his sphere of influence.

The reason Russia wanted to hijack Burisma was stupid-simple: natural gas. John McCain said it best: "Russia is a gas station masquerading as a country." Without oil and gas, the Russian economy, in terms of GDP, would rank just ahead of that of Illinois among the fifty states. Putin's power comes from his control over natural assets, particularly energy—along with Russia's estimated 6,800 nuclear warheads.

It would be easy to look at Zlochevsky and say that he's part of the problem. But you have to start somewhere. It was a time of crisis in Ukraine. No matter how imperfect the entity I was asked to champion, I knew one thing, which Kwasniewski had underscored so forcefully: Burisma was opposed to the direct interests of the most dangerous person in the world—Vladimir Putin.

If I was going to pick a side—and if I was going to get paid to pick a side—I'd choose the same way again, rather than back the person President Trump has sided with.

After gathering all that background, Boies Schiller recommended that Burisma go even further in following Western standards of corporate transparency and governance and that it look to diversify, in partnership with international companies around the globe.

Besides Kwasniewski, the board included other respected heavyweights. Alan Apter, an American investment banker based in London, had advised companies throughout Eastern Europe. Joseph Cofer Black, who would join the board in 2016, was director of the CIA's Counterterrorist Center during the George W. Bush administration.

There's no question my last name was a coveted credential. That has always been the case—do you think if any of the Trump children ever tried to get a job outside of their father's business that his name wouldn't figure into the calculation? My response has always been to work harder so that my accomplishments stand on their own.

Still, I was absolutely qualified to do what Burisma needed done. As is true with many boards, I wasn't brought in to give expert advice in areas where the company already had experts—in this case, natural gas. My charge instead was to do what Boies Schiller recommended: make sure Burisma further implemented corporate practices that were up to accepted ethical snuff. Burisma wasn't starting from zero; it didn't appear to be some idle oligarch's plaything. It's an incredibly well-run company.

Am I an expert in corporate governance? Did I have experience and contacts around the world?

While an unpaid chair of World Food Program USA, which the U.S. supported through six different agencies, I helped increase funding 60 percent in five years—to more than $2 billion. For my work there and at other nonprofits, including Catholic Charities and Bono's One Campaign, I interacted with government and business officials in too many countries to count: Jordan, Syria, Lebanon, Kenya, Djibouti—the list goes on. While at Amtrak, I helped spearhead the search for a new president, with the promise of negotiating a union contract for the first time in eight years. As a director in the Department of Commerce during the late 1990s, focusing on e-commerce, I traveled often with then-secretary William M. Daley, everywhere from Uruguay to Cairo to Vietnam to Ghana. I traveled so much for my own consulting business and had contacts in places so wide-ranging that my elevator pitch to clients was that we could help build their portfolio "from Baltimore to Beijing."

So, yes, I brought something besides my name to the Burisma board's table.

My association was transparent and widely reported on from the start. Burisma put out a press release about my appointment, and within a week the *Wall Street Journal* ran a news story. That's when Dad called and said, "I hope you know what you're doing," wanting to make sure I'd done the due diligence and legwork necessary to make certain I was on the right side of things.

I assured him I had. I'd been involved in overseas enterprises throughout his two terms as vice president—since I had to stop lobbying for the interests of Jesuit universities and others—and no one at Burisma had even hinted at wanting me to influence the administration. The fact is, there was almost nowhere in the world that didn't somehow cross my father's spheres of influence.

The executive director of Citizens for Responsibility and Ethics in Washington, a nonprofit government watchdog group, told a reporter at the time, "It can't be that because your dad is the vice president you can't do anything."

The irony, of course, is that my name's weight in Ukraine came from my dad's position as point man for the administration's push to get the country to clean up its act. Both U.S. and international support for Ukraine, and for the pro-Western president who replaced Yanukovych, was pegged to rooting out corruption. In many instances, that corruption was tied directly to Putin's growing influence.

A priority for my dad was the ouster of the country's prosecutor general, Viktor Shokin, for his failure to adequately investigate corruption. It was a view shared widely by European allies. Among the high-profile companies that Shokin was criticized for not pursuing: Burisma.

What came into focus for me after looking into Burisma was just how high a priority the takeover of Ukraine's energy sector had become for Russia. As Kwasniewski had detailed to me during his initial pitch, Russia appeared to be attacking Burisma as much as it was assailing Ukraine.

That assessment has since been validated by any number of revelations.

It came to light that Russian military spies attempted to hack Burisma in the fall of 2019, in search of dirt on me and my father. Their raid on Burisma's servers and emails coincided with last November's congressional impeachment inquiry into Trump, which centered on whether he strong-armed Ukrainian president Volodymyr Zelensky into announcing a probe of Burisma and me. Trump backed that threat by withholding nearly $400 million in approved military aid and putting Ukrainian lives at risk. The Russian culprits belonged to the same spy agency that hacked the Democratic Party servers and Hillary Clinton's campaign chairman, John Podesta, in 2016.

Meanwhile, Giuliani's rogue dirt-finding mission on behalf of the president unraveled almost daily. Texts and documents supplied by Giuliani's Ukrainian American point man, Lev Parnas, revealed just how low and compromised those overseas dealings have been— and underscore why Trump adopted my name as a rallying cry to divert attention from his own. These include notes Parnas took while speaking to Giuliani by phone in a hotel in Vienna. One was an almost comically clear reference to their effort to get "Zalensky" (as Parnas spelled his name in the note) to announce investigations into my dad. In fact, it said almost exactly that: "Get Zalensky to Announce that the Biden case will Be Investigated."

Among Parnas's many blockbuster revelations, one of the most damning was Giuliani's connection to Dmytro Firtash, a Ukrainian oligarch whom U.S. federal prosecutors have described in court papers as an associate of Russian organized crime (which he denied). More charitable descriptions of Firtash include a "Kremlin influence agent" and, from a Ukrainian parliamentarian who investigated him, "a political person representing Russian interests in Ukraine." It has also been reported that Firtash is attached to Semion Mogilevich, believed to be the Russian Mafia's "boss of bosses." He sat on the FBI's Ten Most Wanted Fugitives list.

Firtash also appears to be the person with whom Giuliani reportedly tried to cut a deal, promising to get the U.S. Department of Justice to drop its attempt to extradite him to the United States on bribery charges.

Whether or not everything Parnas alleges turns out to be true is hardly the point. In the words of one *New York Times* columnist, "The very fact that a person like Parnas was carrying out high-level international missions for the president shows how mob-like this administration is."

That's why Burisma considered my last name gold. As Kwasniewski has since said: "I understand that if someone asks me to be part of some project it's not only because I'm so good; it's also because I am Kwasniewski and I am a former president of Poland. And this is all interconnected. No-names are a nobody. Being a Biden is not bad. It's a good name."

To put it more bluntly: having a Biden on Burisma's board was a loud and unmistakable fuck-you to Putin.

I joined the board in April 2014.

Every organization's board dynamics differ. They can be combative during times of crisis, leadership upheavals, or a looming takeover. Boards can act as referees or change agents. In the case of Burisma, we were largely guardrails, there in case operations veered off track, agendas diverted from the norm—or events blew up again with Russia.

Burisma ran like a machine, with the palpable confidence of a business that had plenty of room to grow. The board gathered twice a year for meetings or energy forums, in various locations around Europe. Concerns or disagreements that might arise about organizational decisions were worked out ahead of time. We received regular communications about hires, ongoing and potential projects, and other company matters, then signed off on them as needed. At meetings, we approved resolutions required by the charter and assisted in initiating ideas for expansion.

The company culture is both accomplished and nerdy. That springs from Zlochevsky. There is no not noticing him: he's pure mass wrapped in tailored suits and gentlemanly manners. His jowly face holds an almost permanent smirk, which would be disconcerting if it didn't so often seem directed at himself. He doesn't suffer fools lightly.

He speaks primarily Russian and Ukrainian, not English. At board meetings, a translator sat behind soundproof glass while members wore headphones like those you see in the General Assembly of the United Nations. Yet during our board dinners, with his translator always seated beside him, Zlochevsky was not a big conversationalist or storyteller. He was a listener. Kwasniewski, who spoke Polish, Russian, Ukrainian, and English (and probably six other languages as well), regaled us with behind-the-scenes insights and colorful political histories from bygone days in Poland. Apter elucidated for us the reality of Brexit and the sustainability of the EU. Zlochevsky, meanwhile, merely leaned forward in rapt attention. He zeroed in on everybody like that—right down to the waiters.

Zlochevsky is an energy wonk. He's most animated when talking about the geology, engineering, and heavy machinery behind Burisma's drilling operations. He's meticulous about details associated with his processing plants: their systems, their cleanliness. He loves to show off videos, filmed with drones, that give a bird's-eye view of how the vast network of pipes used to extract gas fits together. His closest friends are the company's young engineers and others at Burisma who do the actual hands-on work.

He isn't just a cold technocrat, however. When he was ecology minister, Zlochevsky championed the end to the longstanding practice in Ukraine of chaining bears held in captivity in open pits. It was a politically unpopular stance, but he persevered and won reforms.

He was incredibly kind to me when Beau died. Two months after the funeral, Zlochevsky moved Burisma's board meeting to a fishing lodge at the top of Norway, where the continental shelf breaks. The move was prompted by an offhand comment I'd once made about how Beau's son loved to fish. Zlochevsky told me to bring little Hunter along, and I did, along with my daughter Maisy, who's always up for an adventure.

It was during summer and the endless white nights. For three days we'd drop a line thirty meters down with nine hooks at different levels and pull out nine fish. Little Hunter and Maisy jumped off a dock into the ice-cold water, then got out and jumped into hot-spring baths. I mostly kept to myself—more, I think, than Zlochevsky would have liked—but we all had an enormous amount of fun together, up there at the top of the world. I appreciated his thoughtfulness.

My work for Burisma centered on monitoring corporate practices and suggesting improvements whenever they seemed necessary. As an additional responsibility, I took on business development and expanding the company's operations. I wanted the rest of the world to see that Burisma could operate responsibly outside of Ukraine.

I advocated for a geothermal project in Italy and efforts to be part of the pipeline and drilling operations in Kazakhstan. When Pemex, the state-owned petroleum company in Mexico, opened the door for partners to privatize drilling operations in the Eagle Ford rock formation in the northern part of the country, I supplied connections in Mexico City from my previous business dealings there, then flew down to arrange meetings.

Burisma was good at what it did and getting better at doing more. That's what I tracked, encouraged, and promoted.

And for that, my name became a Trump campaign rallying cry that brought in millions in T-shirt sales.

Where's Hunter?! Twenty-five bucks! Sizes small to 3XL!

*　　*　　*

Did I make a mistake by taking a seat on the board of a Ukrainian gas company?

No.

Did I display a lack of judgment?

No.

Would I do it again?

No.

I did nothing unethical, and have never been charged with wrongdoing. In our current political environment, I don't believe it would make any difference if I took that seat or not. I'd be attacked anyway. What I do believe, in this current climate, is that it wouldn't matter what I did or didn't do. The attacks weren't intended for me. They were meant to wound my dad.

He understands that, of course, far better than I do. Whenever I apologized to him for bringing so much heat onto his campaign, he responded by saying how sorry he was for putting me on the spot, for bringing so much heat onto me, especially at a time when I was so determined to get well.

That's the biggest political debate my dad and I had for months: Who should apologize to whom?

My only misjudgment was not considering, back in 2014, that in three years Trump would sit in the White House, where he would employ every scorched-earth tactic at his disposal to remain there.

Knowing all of that now: No, I would not do it again. I wouldn't take the seat on Burisma's board. Trump would have to look elsewhere to find a suitable distraction for his impeachable behavior.

There was, however, a more unintentional consequence to my stint with Burisma. The fallout was far darker, in its way, than any of the nonsense Giuliani dreamed up.

Burisma turned into a major enabler during my steepest skid into addiction. While its robust compensation initially gave me more time and resources to look after my brother, it played to the worst aspects of my addictive impulses after his death. Burisma wasn't my sole source of income during that period. I was a mostly functional addict until near the very end; I kept clients for longer than one might think possible, and I had money from investments made elsewhere over the years.

But by that mad, bad end, the board fee had morphed into a wicked sort of funny money. It hounded me to spend recklessly, dangerously, destructively.

Humiliatingly.

So I did.

CHAPTER SEVEN

CRACKED

About four months after I got back from Esalen, I dove into the kind of next-level bingeing few addicts see coming.

I'd stayed sober since shortly after that drunken barricade in my apartment. I was a steadfast outpatient at a rehab clinic in Washington, where the staff tested me regularly for alcohol and drugs. I was getting my health back, ate well, and attended a yoga class every day, all while rejoining the real world by consulting for five or six major clients.

Then, over Memorial Day weekend 2016, I flew to Monte Carlo to attend a meeting of the Burisma board. I felt strong enough by then to bring along my oldest daughter, Naomi, presenting the trip to her as a gift for graduating earlier that month from Penn.

The weekend quickly turned contentious—then disastrous. The board meeting itself was unremarkable and mostly pro forma. However, I soon stepped on a stage to discuss global economics with a panel of esteemed, never-met-an-opposing-opinion-they-couldn't-dismiss economists and former ministers of finance from across Europe.

My first mistake: saying what I meant. My second mistake: being right about it.

I posited an opinion that the referendum on Brexit, to be held in the United Kingdom in just a few weeks, had a damn good chance of passing. Conventional wisdom held that Brexit was a long shot. But conventional wisdom was dissolving with the rise of far-right populism around the world, including in Poland, Brazil, and France. In the U.S., Trump had become the GOP's presumptive presidential nominee. It didn't take a psychic to see where things were headed. All you had to do was stick a finger in the air to gauge the winds of change.

I didn't argue that Brexit was a wise choice for the UK. But as with similar movements elsewhere, that didn't appear to matter. I put the odds at better than even that the Brits would cut off their nose to spite their face and vote to eject from the European Union, despite what seemed like the prevailing view to the contrary. Yet my fellow panelists, who'd invested their careers in establishing and preserving the EU, would have none of it. Basically, they called me crazy.

I could've just let it roll off my back and moved on. Or I could've responded more diplomatically. Instead, when the group of graybeard wise men dismissed my Brexit handicapping with what I took to be patronizing arrogance—*What does an American know?*—I pulled my finger out of the air and stuck it, metaphorically, in the esteemed panel's collective eyeball.

The discussion quickly turned combative, then bordered on ugly. I spotted Naomi squirming in the audience.

I got through it but reached for a couple of drinks afterward. That night, while Naomi went off with Zlochevsky's daughter, I wandered into the hotel nightclub and drank some more. Monte Carlo provides a temptation for any taste. When I went to the restroom, someone offered me cocaine.

I took it.

I regretted the slip immediately. When we returned to the States, I went straight to the clinic and confessed to my counselors what I'd done. I even discussed it at that day's group session. I saw my relapse as a troubling but hardly irreversible setback. I was still committed to recovery.

Then a counselor told me he had to inform Kathleen of what had happened—that was the deal cut when I started there. He also said I needed to take a drug test, even though I'd just admitted what I'd done. Kathleen and I had been separated for close to a year and our divorce was imminent. The drug test was not covered by the privacy guidelines in HIPAA and could be used in court against me. I felt ambushed. I refused to take the drug test while continuing to own up to what I'd done. I didn't want it on paper. I just wanted to get better.

The debate grew heated. A counselor at another clinic had already told my daughters months earlier that if they spoke with me they'd be complicit in my death—in my mind, an infuriating breach. So I was working with a short fuse anyway. That fuse was then lit by the clinic's stubborn insistence on a drug test to prove something I'd openly conceded.

I stormed out of the building. And like any proper addict or alcoholic, I embraced my resentment to stoke my addiction.

That, in a nutshell, is addict-think.

I jumped on the bike I'd ridden there and headed straight to an area near Franklin Square, at Fourteenth Street and K, a longtime drug bazaar blocks from the White House. It was a warm late afternoon and the streets were mostly cleared out. It didn't take me long to spot the person I was looking for:

Bicycles.

Almost anyone who lives or works in DC has at one time or another seen Bicycles—also known as Rhea, a homeless, middle-aged Black woman—weaving in and out of traffic or swerving around sidewalk pedestrians on a mountain bike that looks three times too big for her. She usually sports a backpack and a baseball cap, and has a sharp, piercing voice that can be heard a block away as she shouts for everybody to get the hell out of her way, which she does almost continuously. (Because I believe Rhea still lives on the streets, I'm using a pseudonym for her.)

I first met Rhea sometime around my senior year at Georgetown. I'd been out drinking with friends one night, got into a foul, to-hell-with-it mood, and broke off from the pack in the middle of the night to visit this same park. It was at the height of the crack epidemic, in the early 1990s, and with a fledgling addict's wrongheaded sense of misadventure, I decided to see what all the hubbub was about.

A crackhead seemed to spontaneously generate in front of me. He asked what I was looking for. I told him I wanted some "hard," the street term for crack cocaine. He said sure, just give him $100, he'd be right back. I called bullshit: I wasn't some naïve college bro, or at least that's what I tried to project. The guy said no problem, he'd leave behind one of his shoes to ensure his return. That made a certain 2 a.m. sense to me: Who'd take off without returning for his shoe? He assured me he'd be back with my request in no time.

I stood there in the pitch black, in a park you wouldn't want to loiter around in the middle of the day, let alone the middle of the night, and waited—gripping his ratty old shoe.

Ten minutes later, with the crackhead long gone, this tiny Black woman, a few years older than me but looking twice my age, rolled up on a bike with a shoe that matched the one I was still holding.

"You stupid motherfucker," she said in a loud, exasperated tone. "You fell for one of the oldest cons in the book. You stupid . . ."

"Who the fuck are you?" I shot back.

I tried to maintain my streetwise pose. It must have been laughable.

Bicycles then explained with a kind of world-weary patience that dealers often keep old, thrown-away shoes hidden nearby to rip off easy marks like me. To prove her point, she'd retrieved a shoe the crackhead had stashed away.

I stood there like the dumb, gullible college bro I was. Bicycles then sold me what little crack she had on her, and told me to get the hell out.

"You going to get hurt, boy."

*   *   *

Fast-forward two decades later:

After storming out of the clinic, I spotted Bicycles wheeling by, motioned for her to come over, and asked if she could get me some hard. Since my days at Georgetown, I'd handed her change or bills when I saw her on the street and we'd become passing acquaintances. Washington can be a small town like that. More recently, since I'd moved into my apartment, she occasionally rode by my second-story window and called out to see if I needed anything. She'd take whatever money I threw down, buy me cigarettes or whatever else I needed from a nearby 7-Eleven, and keep what was left for herself.

Bicycles's response to my request for "hard" this time was flat and knowing:

"You don't want to do that."

Bicycles is a decades-long user, not a dealer; whatever she sold she did only to make enough money to buy. But I persisted. She didn't require much convincing. She needed my money as much as I needed her access to drugs; she'd take my $100 to buy ten dime bags, hand over eight, and keep two for herself. The relationship was symbiotic: we'd exchange money and drugs despite the fact that each of us sincerely wished the other didn't use. It was two crack addicts who couldn't find their way out of a paper bag.

A one-act crack farce.

After going through those ritual motions of concern, Rhea snapped the $100 from my hand, pedaled off, and returned minutes later with what I wanted.

I'm not exactly sure of the sequence of events that followed. But I do remember that the first hits I took resulted in only a slightly better bang than I got that time back in college. Then, like now, I pushed the small rock of crack into the tip of a cigarette and lit it up.

Like most things one wants to become successful at, smoking crack requires practice and the right tools. I returned to the same spot the next day, and this time Rhea arrived with the works: crack, a pipe, and a screen. She also gave me a brief tutorial to make sure I took a proper hit.

I spotted a chair half hidden by a pillar in front of a closed coffee shop. I settled in, lifted the pipe to my lips, lit the rock, and inhaled. In an instant, I experienced what's called a "bell ringer"—crack's holy grail.

The sensation is one of utter, almost otherworldly well-being. You are at once energetic, focused, and calm. Blood rushes to every extremity; your skin ripples with what feels like bumblebees. Eyes get jangly yet stay alert. Eardrums compress to the point that every sound pours through with such intensity—like a shot through a rifle barrel—that you think you're having auditory hallucinations. You're actually just hearing with hypersensitivity—you're a field dog. You pick up the merest peep from a block away.

I chased that high, on and off, for the next three years.

If the intent when reaching for that first hit is to anesthetize yourself so you won't feel the hurt or shame you felt just moments before, then crack is your new best friend.

After that first bell ringer, I smoked it every day for the next two weeks. It was, indeed, my new best friend; booze was now like an old high school buddy I still got together with but saw less of as time went on. I spent a couple of thousand dollars on crack in those first two weeks, with Rhea serving as my conduit. Before I knew it, I was all in. In the big, bad world of functional substance abuse, as practiced in polite society, I'd crossed what for many is an unfathomable line. I knew it as I crossed it. I'd lift a crack pipe to my mouth, flick the lighter with my thumb, and before inhaling think, *What the fuck!*

But my new best friend turned more and more demanding. Addiction's most self-defeating algorithm: if you're numbing your-self against acute feelings of emptiness or trauma or self-loathing, those feelings will double in intensity as each high tails off.

The antidote is simple: more. Yet the more of the drug you use, the less effective it becomes—the less bang that you and your self-worth get for your buck. There's an antidote for that, too: *lots* more. The power of not feeling, if only for increasingly fleeting seconds, remains the only power you have.

Crazy as it sounds, a substance abuser often feels like a smarter version of a non-abuser. I wasn't a sloppy or mean drunk; I wasn't an addled or dangerous crackhead. Whether it's genetic or physiological, I have the capacity and tenacity to use to excess, and a single-minded unwillingness to quit. That makes addiction easy rather than hard. I had figured out how not to feel bad while still going on about my business. I couldn't comprehend how people who weren't addicts didn't understand how great crack cocaine is. I mean, if you knew how good it made you feel, maybe you wouldn't look at me like I had three heads.

Of course, it's all delusional and self-defeating—but not at the moment. At the moment, you can do crack around the clock, every day, and still make your meetings (sometimes), still return your calls (sometimes), still pay your bills (sometimes).

And when you can't do those things? There's always crack to make you feel not so bad about it.

Here's the thought you never have:

Put. The. Pipe. Down.

Crack is just an answer. It's not *the* answer, but it's the most obvious answer to the question non-abusers ask addicts all the time.

Them: Why do you do drugs?

Us: Because they make me feel good.

All that was ahead.

Rhea eventually moved into my apartment and stayed for about five months.

It was raining cats and dogs one evening when she stopped by under my window to see if there was anything I needed. She was soaking wet, and I insisted she come inside. She lugged her bike up to the second floor, saw a mattress in my empty second bedroom, and fell asleep there.

The next morning, I went to work and left a spare key. When I came home, she was still there and nothing was missing. Three days later, she was there still. Five days later, I cut her her own set of keys.

She never officially moved in; I never officially said, "Take the spare bedroom." But she didn't move out until I moved out.

I know it sounds insane. Yet I also knew Rhea was smart enough, and had been on the streets long enough, to realize she had a good thing. She was the most honest crook I've ever known. She'd call me at work and start the conversation with "I found some of your credit cards . . ." Or: "I didn't steal your ATM card. I took it. The difference between stealing and taking is me telling you I used them. I won't ever lie."

"Rhea," I'd say with a sigh, "we have to get over that."

Rhea is also the funniest person I know, as well as the most eccentric. She's plagued by obsessive-compulsive behavior from her years of addiction. She dresses in clean, well-maintained clothes and always smells fresh—or fresh-ish. She showers twice a day when she can and brushes her teeth and cleans her nails obsessively. She has slept on the subway for days or even weeks, using a small public storage unit to stow her clothes, which she keeps compulsively tidy. Inside my apartment, she watched only true-crime shows, feeding a paranoia that slipped into something more acute when she smoked too much and went too long without sleep.

One TV episode detailed the story of a clinically insane guy who broke into houses, lived in the walls, then killed everybody. He was eventually caught but escaped from prison. I was in L.A. when Rhea watched it, and she called me in a panic. When I got home, she'd put tape over my door's peephole, as if passersby could peek *in*. She was certain the wall-living maniac was still on the loose and about to show up any minute.

Rhea told me endless stories about her childhood. She was raised in her grandmother's house in southeast Washington, DC, near RFK Stadium, and so was a Washington football fan. Neither parent was around and there was little supervision. She was . . . mischievous. She'd sneak into the police precinct station, loiter around the lobby, then crawl beneath a bench and spend the night. Other times she slept in the backs of parked police cruisers, hiding in the rear footwell and riding around without the cops knowing. She once saw a Prince concert after sneaking into the arena two days before the show and sleeping under the bleachers.

When she was around sixteen, she decided to go to Tampa to see Washington play in the Super Bowl. She slipped onto a train bound for Florida and made it all the way to Norfolk. A porter spotted her as she headed to the dining car. When he asked for her ticket, Rhea said her parents had it. "Honey," the porter said before turning her over to authorities at the next station, "you and I are the only two Black people on this train. So I don't know who you think your parents are."

When she got older, Rhea lived for two years in motel rooms she never paid for. She sneaked into the rooms as cleaning ladies finished up, then slid under the bed before the guests returned, staying there through the night.

This was at the height of the crack epidemic, and Rhea got swept right up. Violence was out of control, and women living on the street were especially vulnerable, day and night, to sexual assaults.

She told me she had seven children, one on death row, another in prison for life. She didn't know the whereabouts of the five others. I overheard her talking on a phone once or twice with a sister who lived in the area, but that appeared to be the extent of their relationship.

When Rhea didn't have a place to stay, she had buildings she could sneak into and sleep in the stairwells. There was an apartment in a public housing complex that she sometimes rotated into and out of with a couple of other people, staying as a guest as long as she could. She had to check in at the guard stand out front, where they kept track of visits, and she'd constantly get in arguments there over whether she'd exceeded the number of times she could go in.

Rhea avoided the police like the plague. She hadn't been arrested in a long time, but she told me she had priors—petty crimes, creeping into houses, usually of people she knew—and she was such a known entity on the streets that she was scared to death of being sent away for a long time for some trivial bullshit. I never saw her so much as shoplift.

Rhea survived for decades on streets that lose people every day. She could be a handful, as you might imagine. She had a hair-trigger temper and anger issues, but she also wasn't beyond putting on the persona of a mentally ill madwoman whom other street people wouldn't mess with. It helped keep predators from doing what predators do, which is prey on a little woman who was now an aging little woman.

Among the many maladies associated with her long-term crack use, Rhea suffered from peripheral neuropathy. She told me the painful condition was induced by an allergic reaction she had to cocaine mixed with lidocaine, a numbing agent often used for legitimate purposes as a nerve block. She'd lose feeling in her extremities: fingers, toes, nose, the tips of her ears. When the weather turned cold or she smoked too much, her nose and ears blew up like balloons.

Now Rhea was living with me. I was gone much of the time, traveling for family, or business, or just trying to disappear. But when I was home, the two of us interacted like a deranged, crack-addled version of *The Odd Couple*, her Felix Unger neatnik habits crashing against my slobbier Oscar Madison tendencies.

She commandeered the TV and only watched those true-crime shows, with the volume turned way up. It drove me insane. I'd wear headphones, or pace the room and shout for her to turn the damn thing down. The angriest I ever got at her was when she took a belt I loved and cut it in half to fit her size-nothing waist. Rhea weighed maybe eighty-five pounds soaking wet.

I probably bugged her more than she bugged me. She got mad when I left dirty clothes on the coffee table or spilled vodka on a rug. When I wasn't traveling, she left the apartment more than I did; after so many years on the streets, being confined inside for too long made her itchy and claustrophobic.

That time on the streets took its toll, of course. She'd limp from an infection in her ankle, or arthritis would flare up in her hips. Sometimes bursitis almost immobilized her; the pain she had to endure just to get up could be excruciating. I'd take her to an emergency room if it became unbearable. Otherwise, I'd go to a CVS to pick up prescriptions she got from a clinic, antibiotics for whatever infection she was prone to.

It was heartbreaking.

Mainly, however, we just planted ourselves on the couch and smoked a ton of crack. For endless hours, day after day, it was the same numbing ritual, over and over and over: pipe, Chore Boy, crack, light; pipe, Chore Boy, crack, light; pipe, Chore Boy, crack, light.

A world of previously invisible commonplace objects became indispensable accoutrements to our sacramental routine. The pipe we used most often, called a stem, was actually a made-in-China glass tube that comes with a decorative paper rose inside. Sold as a tchotchke and referred to as a "glass rose," it's used to smoke crack. The tube is the same length and width as a 100-millimeter cigarette, and so can be carried surreptitiously in a pack of cigarettes.

Chore Boy is a spun-copper scouring pad. Packaged in orange boxes displaying a cartoon boy wearing blue overalls and a backward-facing red cap, Chore Boy is designed to clean pots and pans. Addicts, who call it "choy," use it as a screen to hold the crack in their rose pipes. Rhea always lit the choy first to burn off any chemicals.

At DC bodegas frequented by addicts, clerks conveniently hand you a pipe and choy together when you order a "one-and-one."

Archmere Academy, Georgetown, Yale Law—and here I was, ecstatic with my new knowledge of rose pipes, Chore Boy, and one-and-one.

Smoking with Rhea was a master class in crackology. She had a million rules: Always know where your shit is. Always recook your crack if you got it from someone you don't know to burn off the trash some dealers mix in. Never stick your stem in your pants pocket, where it can break when you sit or fall out of your pants while you're ordering at Popeyes.

She often pointed out rites of passage in my crack addiction, even numbering and abstracting them, like a lecturer in an advanced independent-study course.

#37: Loses apartment keys whenever he goes out.

#67: Never picks eyes up from the floor more than thirty seconds at a time because always scanning floor for crack crumbs.

At one point, she said I'd graduated into crackology's PhD program. It was during the phase when it took me an eternity just to pack a bag for a trip. I'd have a flight in two hours, and two days later I'd still be sitting in the apartment, bag open and clothes strewn everywhere. Rhea would walk in and shake her head. "Are you fucking kidding me? Here," she'd say, and grab my clothes, stuff them in the bag, and push me out the door.

Rhea saved me, even as she sucked me in. She wouldn't let me buy from anyone else, protecting me from having to track down my own drugs on DC's more cutthroat streets. She taught me how to use as safely as possible. She was meticulous about who she bought from, where she bought it, and what was good stuff and what was trash. She always bought in reasonable increments that, in theory at least, limited me from going on a full-out binge—meaning, in the relative insanity of that universe, not using continuously for more than two or three days straight. (Later, on my odysseys through California and Connecticut, two- and three-day binges would seem quaint.)

I loved Rhea as much as I've ever loved a friend. She's the only person from that period of my life I actively maintain good memories of. During my years of addiction, I learned this: mean drunks and addicts are mean people, violent drunks and addicts are violent people, and stupid drunks and addicts start out as stupid people. Rhea was none of those. There are embarrassing, shameful, even shocking things we've all done while high. Yet there is a line that the best won't cross, no matter how desperate: hurting someone. Rhea wouldn't hurt a fly.

Rhea breaks my heart more than any friend I've ever had. Wicked smart, stand-up-comedian funny, resourceful, damaged—she's been pedaling through a haze of survival and drug addiction for so long that she's scared to death to put down the crack pipe. She has no relationship with her family, doesn't have anyone in her daily life who loves her genuinely and unconditionally. She has no memory of any beauty awaiting her on the other side.

It would be a miracle if Rhea was ever able to get clean. But by the mere fact that I'm sitting here and writing about her, I'm a miracle. One day I hope to be strong enough to go back to see Rhea, in that very dark place she resides, and do what I can to get her in a position where she wants to be saved. I don't want Rhea to believe that things will get better only by her dying.

Until then, her lesson is stark and unrelenting and holy: we're all just human beings, trying as hard as we fucking can.

CHAPTER EIGHT

INTO THE DESERT

In October 2016, I set out on a crack-fueled, cross-country odyssey.

That wasn't my plan. The plan was to get well. Until a couple of months earlier, I'd limited my crack use to once every three days. I believed I could quit it on my own, whenever I wanted, before it devolved into a full-time disorder. I was driving back and forth between DC and Delaware to see Hallie and her kids, our relationship still just a shared-grief oasis, and tried to keep my drug use hidden.

But I was also traveling for work constantly, mostly to generate new clients and trying to keep existing ones. My drug use accelerated in tandem with my stress. Smoking crack cocaine every three days soon became smoking every two days, then every other day—then every hour of every day. While still fairly new to the around-the-clock use of crack—and still learning how to be a functional abuser at that enhanced scale of addiction; still learning how to excuse myself in the middle of meetings every twenty or thirty minutes to light up in the men's room—I knew I needed to do something before it spun out of control.

At least that's what I told myself.

I was quick to deflect any notions that I was in extreme distress, that there was anything awry beyond my drinking, which had become more blatant as my anger rose over a dissolving marriage and the separation from my daughters. I avoided family and friends who were most likely to spot it. That included my dad. I didn't want my family to confront me and insist I return to a rehab center that I'd been to before. I knew that wouldn't do me any good right now. I was entering a new realm—a new level of darkness.

Following a relapse and my discharge for failing a drug test after an embarrassingly short stint in the U. S. Navy Reserve, I had rehabbed in 2014 at a clinic in Tijuana, where I was treated with a plant-derived psychoactive called ibogaine—legal in Mexico and Canada but not in the United States. A woman there knowledgeable about alternative therapies told me about a wellness ranch in Sedona, Arizona.

Grace Grove Retreat is run by a couple who are devoted New Agers—the woman goes by the name Puma St. Angel, a moniker she told me was given to her years earlier by a shaman. It sounded like a spot that might be just different enough, just alternative enough, and just potentially effective enough to help get me well. It was more of a holistic detox center for stressed-out executives than a drug rehab clinic. It offered treatments such as liver and gallbladder cleanses, meditation and yoga classes, and hikes through the spectacular red-rock terrain that surrounded the center. I saw it as a place where I could reorder myself and get healthy.

I arranged to meet up there with a friend named Joseph Magee, whom I'd met during my first stay at Crossroads, in 2003. We'd remained close. Originally from east Texas, where in the late 1990s he helped stage a controversial college production of *Angels in America*, and now a successful businessman in New York with his fashion-company-owning husband, Joey was a recovering addict who'd helped me and countless others through many trying times. He was also a bit of a rehab junkie—he'd been to about forty different rehabs, no exaggeration, and was beloved everywhere he went—and was always willing to come to a friend's aid at a moment's notice.

This time was no different. I just called him and said, "Hey, Joe, I'm going to this crazy fucking wellness ranch in Sedona. You want to come?"

His reply: "I'll meet you there."

I asked Joey to join me because I knew I wouldn't want to let him down. Left to giving my recovery over to a pair of strangers, I'd likely as not hit eject before getting there by employing my default evasion in such circumstances: *Fuck it.* Joey would be my fuck-it insurance.

I had become resistant to traditional twelve-step-based rehabilitation—or too burned out on it, or too proficient at gaming it—for that method alone to seem like much use. It had worked for me for extended periods in the past, and there's much about it I believe is invaluable—I still employ many of its tenets to stay sober. But addiction is so complex, so individual, and dependent on so many factors that combating it can often make an addict feel like a rat in a maze, continuously searching for solutions while bumping into barriers that keep him or her from staying clean.

It's a maze in which too many alcoholics and addicts find themselves trapped. Relapse rates for rehabilitation centers hover between 60 and 80 percent, a distressing volume of failure for a $40 billion industry into which abusers and their families pour so much time, money, and emotional currency.

The truth is, by my midforties, I had learned every lesson I needed to learn. Now I was learning how to ignore them. There were more pertinent matters for me to master: the most efficient ways to buy and smoke crack; how best to hide my use.

Those were the sorts of things I became hyperfocused on—not my failures at attempting to get clean but my successes in buying and using without getting caught or hurt or killed during some random drug-buy mix-up. Walking into a park in a high-crime neighborhood to buy crack at 4 a.m. was no different than playing Russian roulette with two shells in the chamber. In some places, it was like playing with five shells—and still, I was willing to spin the chamber again and again.

So off I went to see Puma St. Angel.

I arrived at Dulles International Airport at 7 a.m., three hours before my flight's scheduled departure, a nod to the ridiculous amounts of time it now took me to accomplish even the most mundane tasks. Before getting out of my car at the airport garage, however, I took a hit off a pipe to hold me over. Two hours later, I was still sitting there, still smoking. I decided it didn't matter if I left a little later, that I wasn't on a strict timetable. I'd just take the next flight. When it was too late to catch that one, I resolved to take the next one. A few hours later, I resolved to take the one after that.

I never left my car. Stocked with what I guessed to be enough crack to last a couple of days, I finally missed the last flight of the night. By that point, crackhead wisdom kicked in big-time: I had always wanted to drive across the country, and now seemed a perfect opportunity to do just that. I pulled out of the airport garage around 10 p.m., pointed my car west, and headed toward Arizona, more than 2,200 miles away.

That was day one.

I drove through the night, finally stopping in Nashville a few hours after sunrise. I checked into a hotel and smoked away the rest of the day. By nightfall, I realized I was already running low on drugs. I rummaged through my car seats and floor mats for crumbs, then drove off sometime around midnight to score more.

By now, I possessed a new superpower: the ability to find crack in any town, at any time, no matter how unfamiliar the terrain. It was easy—risky, often frustrating, always stupid and stupendously dangerous, yet relatively simple if you didn't give much of a shit about your own well-being and were desperate enough to have an almost limitless appetite for debasement.

Crack takes you into the darkest recesses of your soul, as well as the darkest corners of every community. Unlike with alcohol, you become dependent not only on a criminal subculture to access what you need but the lowest rung of that subculture—the one with the highest probability of violence and depravity.

Navigating that landscape required me to be absolutely fucking fearless. Almost everybody assumed I was a cop—flashy car, false bravado, white—so I'd often pull out a pipe first and smoke whatever I had in front of them, even if there was only resin left on the screen, just to show I was for real.

Then there was the matter of not getting ripped off. Like cold-calling clients, it was a numbers game of hit-and-miss. I'd either hand $100 to someone to make a buy and wait outside a building as they went in the front door and out the back, or I'd find someone smart enough to figure out that I could be their crack daddy for as long as I was in town. Getting burned became an occupational hazard, a kind of repetitive stress injury: I'd get taken by the same guy, again and again, only to return to hand him money one more time, my desperation for another hit so encompassing that I literally could taste it.

The diciest time to buy was in the predawn morning, stepping into a place where it's inadvisable to be at 4 a.m. with a pocketful of cash and no weapon. You learn little things to protect yourself. You never approach someone before they approach you: You don't want to look too desperate—as if showing up anywhere at 4 a.m. doesn't look desperate enough—because anybody who's in the business of selling crack is in the business of ripping people off. They'll sell you actual rocks from a driveway if you look too needy. When I could, I tried to buy from a user instead of someone who was obviously a dealer. Crack addicts usually came back with something of substance if I also gave them money to get some for themselves, and then promised them more. They had skin in the game. They'd be reliable right up until the point where they got all that they needed and then, almost invariably, they'd rip me off, too.

No honor among us crackheads.

In Nashville, I was a bloodhound on the scent. Like everywhere else I'd bought crack, I knew I could go there cold and in no time assess what highway to get on, what exit to get off at, what gas station to pull into, and what unsavory-looking character to choose as my newest, most trusted associate. I had done it everywhere I'd been the last few months—I could get off a plane in Timbuktu and score a bag of crack.

I followed my usual modus operandi. I headed for a commercial district in the sketchiest part of town and looked for a gas station or liquor store that served as a congregating spot for a quorum of homeless addicts. I'd pull in, stick the nozzle in the gas tank, lock my car, and head inside to buy cigarettes or Gatorade. It rarely took long before somebody out front asked if I could help him out with some change. I'd hand him whatever was in my pocket, then ask for a favor: "You know where I can buy some hard?" The key was finding someone who was homeless because he needed to support his habit, not because he was mentally ill, which was too often the case, and sometimes tough to distinguish.

I found my guy in less than an hour. He was about my age, maybe a little younger, but looked like he'd had a really hard life, at least recently. He was sinewy, had dirty nails but clean sneakers, and wore a dark jacket that looked passable from afar but up close was tattered at the sleeves and hadn't been laundered in a while. He was down on his luck, not plainly homeless but likely on the verge of it.

Yet his eyes burned with the hard, voracious intensity that crack addicts carry into every encounter—and which I also carried into encounters like this one, despite my Porsche and law degree and childhood spent in a Senate sauna listening to the most powerful men in the country call out a hearty "Hey, boys!"

A crack addict's intensity can be intimidating. It feels distinctly predatory, which makes you feel unmistakably like prey. While the drug itself doesn't induce violent behavior, the desperation for more of it most certainly can. Unlike a heroin addict, who, comparatively, luxuriates for a while in his high, a crack addict is scheming shortly after using about only one thing: how to get another hit in the next thirty minutes.

The guy at the gas station that night in Nashville sized me up, too.

"I got Chore Boy. You know what I'm talking about?" he asked with a test in his voice. I told him I did and acted like I was put out by the question. We got in my car. I asked where we were headed.

"I'll let you know," he said in a casual, sandpapery tone. "Just pull out of here."

Our conversation from then on was confined to a series of blunt, robotic bursts.

"Turn right here . . . Now left here."

"What's the address?"

"I don't know the address. I just know where it is."

He told me not to smoke in the car. He told me to buckle my seat belt. "Cops are always up here. They'll arrest you."

He spotted my pipe on the console.

"Anything in here? I'll smoke the resin."

"You just told me not to smoke in the car."

"I know what I'm doing."

It was dark and, except for us, the streets were practically deserted. I had no idea where I was or where we were going. GPS became moot. I kept turning.

He told me to park in front of a run-down, putty-colored two-story apartment building. The way this scenario would usually end is that I would park, give the guy $100 to buy crack, and tell him if he came back I'd give him another $100 to buy for himself. Then I'd wait, like an idiot, at 2 a.m., in the most dangerous part of town. Seven times out of ten he didn't come back. Yet I'd keep waiting anyway, telling myself that it hadn't been all that long. Ten minutes would stretch into an hour, then into an hour and a half. I'd go through elaborate mental gymnastics to justify not leaving. I'd remember a guy I once bought from who came back two hours later.

But mostly they didn't come back: You get burned. You feel ridiculous, you feel pathetic, and then you feel desperate and start all over again, trolling the same gas stations and liquor stores and clubs until finally—at 4 a.m., or 7 a.m., or 10 a.m.—you find a guy who comes through, who actually brings back enough to hold you over for the next four hours, when you'll have to go through the same lousy routine all over again. The process can take thirty minutes or it can take ten hours.

This time, it took thirty minutes. Before I gave the guy my $100, I'd told him to leave behind his Obama Phone—the free cell the federal government started giving to financially strapped Americans during the 2008 recession, under the Lifeline Act. Obama Phones are mocked by conservatives as another liberal scheme to redistribute wealth, yet the legislation was first passed in 1985 by President Reagan to give households access to communications and emergency services through home telephone hookup. That act was merely updated by Obama for a wireless world—to the delight of crack addicts and dealers everywhere.

My guy didn't want to give it up.

"You gotta trust people," he told me with a remarkably straight face.

I thanked him for the life lesson, then told him to leave his cell or there was no deal. He left the phone and ambled off, then returned not long afterward with $100 worth of what he said was crack. You never know. Often it's baking soda or crushed-up pills that somebody has turned into rocks. You light it up and you're high before you even hear the pops—hear the "crack"—whether it's the good stuff or not. The anticipation knocks your socks off; studies have shown, and my experience verifies, that the fiercest rush occurs in the nanoseconds before your lips touch the pipe. It's not until a minute or so later that you can determine whether you're smoking the real deal, and by that time your connection can be out of the car and long gone.

In this case, however, what he brought back was damn good. I'd gotten his phone number off his cell while he was inside, and I turned our late-night one-off into a four-day Nashville run. I called him three or four times a day over that period. He was a godsend for me, and I was the best thing that ever happened to him: over those three days I probably handed him $1,500. The transactions became relaxed, almost matter-of-fact, like dropping in to buy vegetables from the same sidewalk grocer. We hardly ever exchanged a word.

And except for those brief excursions, I stayed holed up in my hotel room with my pipe and my lighter and my crack.

I have to pause here a minute. I apologize. Every neuron in my brain is firing right now, shouting, *Get me more of that! Get me more of that!*

That's what recalling incidents like what I just wrote can trigger. Addicts know what I'm talking about. It's a thin, wobbly line to straddle. While it's important for someone recovering from addiction to speak honestly about what he or she went through, there's also the risk of reigniting those old cravings, which can be fucking monsters.

It's the power of language, for good and for bad. It's the reason characters are afraid to say Voldemort's name aloud in Harry Potter and instead refer to him as He Who Must Not Be Named. They don't want to unleash his dark power over them.

There are times while writing this book when naming the things I've done becomes too much—crack's dark power is unleashed. This is one of those times. Even though my mind realizes that the peace I once got from taking a hit off a crack pipe was temporary and ultimately self-destructive, it also understands that it felt better than the pain I experienced before I took that hit. Crack wasn't the only answer to my ache. But, again, it was an answer, and certainly the most expedient one to that age-old question people won't stop asking:

Why can't you quit?

Because, motherfucker, it feels too good!

So as I write this, I can still feel the hard, hot pipe on my lips, the heat ballooning inside my mouth, the smoke crisping my lungs. I still twitch with the muscle memory of the torch-blast rush that shot to every tip of every appendage of my body. Recalling the events of that night in Nashville, I still get a shiver down my spine.

I can still feel myself seated in my car that late night—the throb in my lower back from those countless hours on the road, the creeping hunch of my shoulders, the racing of my heart—as the guy with the dirty nails and clean sneakers came out of the apartment building with my bag. I can still remember how I fumbled around the side pocket for a lighter and a stem. I can see myself reaching for a new ball of Chore Boy to use as a filter, then deciding to use the old one instead, knowing it was covered in resin and thinking how much better the crack would be if I could draw the smoke through it. I still remember that there were three new stems in a paper bag in the back seat and that I considered reaching around the headrest for one of them. I stopped myself because I thought I'd be better off doling them out, one day at a time, during the rest of my cross-country journey.

I remember I planned to recook the crack back in my hotel

room. Then I tried to remember if I had a spoon to simmer it in, or if there was a microwave in the room I could use to heat it up.

I remember that I couldn't remember.

I still recall that I thought about stopping by a liquor store on the way back to the hotel. Then I realized I could call room service if I needed a drink but then thought about how much more expensive that would be than buying from the store. In the end, I ditched the whole idea, as if my decision not to drink that night was simply a matter of fiscal responsibility. I remember thinking about getting something to eat, too, then thinking, *Fuck it, I have more important matters to attend to.*

What I really remember is getting back to my room at two or three o'clock that morning and stripping off my jacket and settling into a soft chair and pulling out the fresh bag and feeling that first real hit—not the rushed test hit I took earlier in the car with that blazing-eyed stranger looking on hungrily from the passenger seat. And then I remember why I'm remembering all of this: the sensation of being instantly transported—at something like warp speed, as if riding bareback on a rocket ship—to some far-off, beautiful place.

Remembering all of those things feels like a terrible betrayal of where I am now. It induces an urge that's completely counter to how far I've come. When you realize the effect those recollections can have on your mind and body, causing them to work against your deepest desire not to be in that place, you fear their ability to lure you back in. They prompt feelings of shame and guilt that, to be honest, only stir an enhanced sense of hellish excitement.

Addict-think.

I hate it. I hate recalling it. I hate the damage it caused, to me and others. Most of all, I hate still longing for the peace it provided.

It was definitely not one of the beautiful things my brother talked about.

Folks at the wellness ranch in Sedona started blowing up my phone to find out when I'd be arriving. I ignored them. I finally got a call from Joey, who'd checked in days earlier and knew I'd pick up for him. He then put the Grace Grove people on, at their insistence. I minted a new excuse with each call: last-minute business complications, unforeseen family issues.

Joey knew the drill: he understood from his own experience what was going on without my having to tell him. He just stayed the course and waited me out. After four days, I'd already given up on the notion of driving cross-country and booked a flight from Nashville to Phoenix, with a short pit stop in Los Angeles. I'd leave my car in Tennessee and pick it up when I flew back.

I repeated the same sorry routine of smoking and rebooking I'd performed at Dulles. I cloistered myself inside my car at the airport, terrified I'd get busted going through security, or that I couldn't handle the four-hour flight without a hit. I missed one plane after another.

Finally, I boarded a late flight and made it as far as my two-hour layover at LAX. Desperate to smoke, I slipped out of the terminal with my carry-on and whatever drugs I had left and fired up in a parking garage stairwell. I knew I wouldn't make my connecting flight. I phoned Hallie briefly. She alone knew about my trip out west, and I told her what I planned to tell everybody: I'd made it to Sedona and everything was fine.

I stayed that night at a hotel in nearby Marina del Rey, immediately calling a crack connection I'd made during a previous West Coast business trip. I'll call him Curtis here. I'd first found him by using an alternative MO to my superpower: browsing online escort service ads, not for sex but for slipped-in references of offers to "party," which meant, of course, they sold drugs.

Before long, Curtis arrived at the hotel with crack, his prostitute girlfriend, and Honda, a tall, gaunt, affable twentysomething who had been a professional skateboarder until he broke practically every bone in his body. He'd since transitioned to a second career boosting Hondas. During a later stay in L.A., inside a bungalow at the Chateau Marmont, Honda would patiently teach me how to cook my own crack.

My unscheduled pause turned into a six-day bacchanal. Curtis and his crew made my suite their party house, rotating in and out for hours at a time. They blared music, ordered room service, and cleaned out the minibar—all on my dime and with my consent. They took advantage of my largesse but not unreasonably so; I was totally, completely out of my fucking mind. They preferred booze and weed to crack, while I hit the pipe like there was no tomorrow, strolling around in my underwear and generally acting insane.

I never slept. Ever. I made a reservation each day on a puddle jumper from L.A. to Sedona, and each day I canceled it. I couldn't make myself get on a plane.

In time, even the night world's regulars became uneasy. During one mix-up too stupid and tangled to detail, I nearly got in a fight outside an after-hours club on Hollywood Boulevard. Before the club's two massive bouncers could intervene, one of their friends, a Samoan man built like a brick shithouse with braided hair down to his ass, pulled me away to cool me down.

He went by Baby Down, a nickname derived from his older brother, Down—so-called because he could put anybody who hassled him "down" with one punch. You didn't want to mess with Baby Down, either. As I'd learn, he was related to the Boo-Yaa T.R.I.B.E., a local group of Samoan gangsters-turned-rappers whose music became popular in the late 1980s and '90s. Branches from that tree, I was told, had a monopoly on the doormen who worked LA's strip clubs.

That night, Baby Down ushered me to Mel's Drive-In on Sunset and ate and talked with me until I settled down. It felt like a real, rare heart-to-heart. As badass as he looked and likely was, Baby Down seemed empathetic and bright beyond his obvious street smarts. He talked about helping me get cleaned up and back on my feet.

I finally decided to rent a car and drive to Sedona. I left Marina del Rey around four in the morning, on no sleep and in a cavernous Lincoln Town Car, taking I-10 out of California to start the five-hundred-mile jaunt.

I made it as far as San Bernardino, seventy-five miles east. Snow-capped mountains emerged ahead in the breaking twilight.

Exhausted, I checked into a hotel. I still couldn't fall asleep, still couldn't stop smoking. After a while, I got back on the road.

And that should have been that—end of story, end of me.

Around 11 a.m., speeding east along the tabletop-flat highway that unspooled through the baked Sonoran Desert somewhere outside of Palm Springs, the temperature already closing in on ninety degrees, I nodded off behind the wheel. Waking up an instant later, I found myself in midair, the car having jumped a soft curb on the passing lane and soaring at eighty miles an hour into a cloudless blue sky, heading into the gulch that divided I-10.

Nanoseconds unreeled in a kind of stop-action slow motion. I had what seemed like an eternity to size things up and consider my alternatives, even though, of course, I had no time at all. As my car made its descent into the median, I resisted the urge to do what my reflexes were imploring me to do: jam on the fucking brakes! I knew that would cause the Town Car to barrel roll the moment the wheels touched down and then throw me or crush me.

Instead, I hit the gas the second the car landed in the gulch. I let it run for a moment until yanking the steering wheel to avoid a berm that serves as a turnaround for emergency vehicles and the police. The car spun into the westbound lanes—the same direction as the oncoming traffic. Miraculously, there was a gap in the traffic until my car stopped dead in the emergency lane, hissing and coughing. It rested on four flat tires, with cacti and scrub brush wrapped around the undercarriage.

I don't remember how long I sat there. It seemed like forever. I blinked behind sunglasses that had somehow stayed on my head. The luggage in the back seat was now scattered all over the front; the car's interior looked like a war zone. I was shaking, still amped up from being in the middle of my twelve-day roll. Two police cruisers whizzed by without so much as tapping their brakes, like I was somebody who'd pulled over to take a leak or a tourist who'd stopped to ponder the roadside's ceaseless, featureless panorama.

I called the rental company and told them that somebody ran me off the road. The tow truck didn't arrive for a couple of hours, and when the driver looked over the car, I told him that I'd wound up in the gulch. He shrugged.

"Happens all the time," he said before hauling me back to Palm Springs, where I climbed behind the wheel of another rental and continued on to Sedona.

Then things got weird.

I stopped for gas somewhere in the high foothills while driving north through Arizona, rolled back onto the highway, then didn't realize until two hours later that I'd pointed my new Jeep Cherokee in the wrong direction.

Back on the right track, I found myself navigating a winding mountain road beneath a moonless sky well past midnight. There were no lights anywhere. Some sections had guardrails, some did not. I was determined to keep moving rather than pull over and wait until morning. I had called Grace Grove before leaving Palm

Springs and arranged for Joey and Morgan, an ex-cowboy who managed the place with Puma, to pick me up at the rental car office in Prescott, an old western town about an hour and a half's drive from the wellness center.

As the high-desert wind rushed and whistled through the wide-open windows, I played an album of remixes by Mississippi bluesman R. L. Burnside as a kind of propulsive soundtrack. On one song, "It's Bad You Know," Burnside growls those words over and over. I played it almost continuously, like a gonzo incantation. I was out of my fucking mind.

To stay awake, I chain-smoked crack and cigarettes, kept the windows down, and leaned into the bracing night air whenever I felt myself nodding off. At some point, the crack lost its oomph, but I kept lighting up anyway, out of force of habit. Sometimes I just slapped myself in the face.

As I peered ahead into the pitch blackness, at times hunched so far forward my chest bumped against the steering wheel, an enormous barn owl suddenly swooped over my windshield, as if dropped straight from the inky night sky. I looked on in stunned wonder. It glided over the car's hood until it was caught in my high beams. I didn't know if it was real or a hallucination, but it sure as hell woke me up.

Then, as abruptly as it arrived, the bird swerved off to the right, just out of range of my headlights. I swerved with it to stay on the road, and it led me cleanly around a sharp bend. It disappeared for a few minutes after that, as the road straightened, before reappearing again with its massive wings tilting first one way and then the other, guiding me through a series of tight, bounding switchbacks. I just kept following. It did the same thing four or five more times—disappearing, returning, gliding through dips and rises and hairpin turns at full speed, like a stunt plane at an air show, all but beckoning me to stay close behind. I'm not sure how long I followed the owl before it finally led me straight into Prescott. As it flapped off into the star-smeared sky, I shook my head and mouthed a soundless, still-disbelieving "Thank you," over and over and over again.

It was 3 a.m. Joey and Morgan had waited on me for hours. When I pulled in, they weren't amused.

"You won't believe what just happened," I exclaimed, still dumbstruck by what I'd witnessed.

I wanted to recount everything. How I shouldn't even be there. How I'd lucked out in Nashville with a crack dealer who didn't take everything I had at 2 a.m., including my life. How a hustling music impresario wannabe and his girlfriend looked after my best interests and pushed me to clean up instead of robbing me blind. How I didn't kill myself or anyone else after sailing over the highway near Palm Springs. And lastly, how a giant bird—or guardian angel, or figment of my addled imagination—took me under its wings only minutes earlier to keep me from spinning off a mountainside and deliver me here, to this spot, at last.

I wanted to tell them about all of it. But at that hour, in that place, my escorts made it clear they weren't interested in my bullshit.

"Whatever," one of them said, signaling for me to get in the van.

The car's interior was a train wreck; I'd been piloting that rental for ten hellacious hours—smoking, swerving, losing my shit—with the contents of my bag scattered everywhere. Joey and Morgan, rushing to get the hell back, helped me clear it out as best they could. I hopped in the van with them and headed off to get well.

Again.

I didn't leave my bed for the next three days. Detoxing from crack isn't as dangerous as quitting alcohol or as painful as getting off heroin. But a nonstop fourteen-day binge like I'd just gone through leaves the body depleted and dehydrated. Every joint ached like I had severe arthritis; my knees nearly disabled me and I thought the crick in my neck would be permanent. I had a fever and chills and near-panic-level anxiety and on the third day began to continually cough up a disturbing black phlegm. Lying alone in the clean, rustic setting of Grace Grove, with Joey checking in on me every hour and Puma slipping me herbal remedies, the only thing I craved was a crack pipe—the heat filling my mouth, the smoke singeing my lungs, that bareback rocket ride.

I'd left my wallet in the rental car. It contained my brother's AG badge, which I carried everywhere, as well as a Secret Service business card I still had even though I'd canceled my security detail several years earlier. A Hertz employee cleaning out the car found some paraphernalia and a white-powder residue on an armrest. After googling my name and Beau's, the manager called the local police—who called the Secret Service, who called my dad, who, I presume, called Hallie, since she was the only person who knew where I was. I'd left my cell phone in the car, too, so Hallie got in touch with Joey, who took care of things from there. I eventually got everything back.

The Prescott police called Grace Grove to inquire about me but dropped their investigation. I didn't know anything about it until I got out of bed around day four, and dismissed it all as ridiculous. Despite the speculation in the right-wing media to the contrary, the cops weren't strong-armed into dropping the case. As the Prescott city attorney, a man who served twenty years in the Arizona National Guard and had been deployed to Afghanistan, later told the *New Yorker*, "It's a very Republican area. I don't think political favors would even work, had they been requested."

Still, the commotion freaked out the folks at Grace Grove, who knew I was there to recover from drug addiction but had no idea how bad it was. They asked if I had anything on me, worried the cops would show up and nose around. They went through my bag and pulled out all of my drug paraphernalia. Morgan then packed up everything I had and drove off into the high red-rock desert, where he buried it all with a kind of ceremonial earnestness, per the Grace Grove vibe.

He returned to the center several hours later, looking like he'd seen a ghost. His tanned, weathered face was ashen. When I asked what happened, he told me that while burying the instruments of my addiction he'd become violently ill. He then passed out and had apocalyptic visions. His dream's prevailing image, he said: four horsemen wielding scythes atop fire-snorting steeds that were stampeding straight toward me.

I didn't know what the hell to say to that—didn't know whether to laugh or tremble. But the more he talked, the less it mattered. Whether what he saw was prophecy, revelation, or quackery, it struck me as a dead-on metaphor for how I experienced the power of crack and addiction.

Just days earlier, I'd flown over an interstate highway, and only hours after that I'd followed a mammoth bird through pitch-black mountain passes—all to escape the thing that had been chasing me most of my adult life. When I contemplate battling my addiction now, the image I conjure up is of that terrorizing band of skeletal night riders—the Four Horsemen of the Crackocalypse.

I got a lot better during the rest of my stay. I ate properly, meditated, attended a hypnotherapy session, and got cleanses. I didn't smoke crack for the first time in at least fourteen days.

After a week, I left Grace Grove and checked into Mii Amo, a nearby resort spa. Feeling physically and mentally purged, I phoned Hallie and asked if she would come to Arizona to pick me up. I wanted her to accompany me on the trip back. I didn't trust myself to make it home without backsliding—without taking a detour into the pit I fell into on my way there.

She flew out the next day. I was at my lowest, she was at her neediest, and we clung to each other with abandon. We talked at length about how much we had come to rely on each other, how our health and well-being seemed dependent on the love we'd grown to share.

There's no question about the unseen force in the middle of it all: Beau. It seems obvious now, but then it was this unspoken, unacknowledged dynamic that had begun to impel us both: the idea that we could keep Beau alive by being together—that by loving each other we somehow could love him back into existence.

By the time we returned to Delaware at the end of the week, we were no longer just two people bound by shared grief.

We were a couple.

If ever there was a star-crossed coupling, it was ours. It made perfect sense except for how it made no sense at all. We returned from Arizona determined to make a go of it, though I'm not sure either of us understood what that meant. It was an affair built on need, hope, frailty, and doom.

The fact is, Hallie and I weren't close before Beau died. I remember being surprised when Beau married her. As a bachelor, he was much sought after by single women within a thousand-mile radius, and he kept his relationships close to the vest. When Beau lived upstairs in the Delaware house Kathleen and I first bought, Hallie's older sister, whom we knew growing up, came around all the time and Hallie just seemed to tag along. I first saw a connection between her and Beau while he studied for the bar exam, which he had to retake several times (the Delaware bar is notoriously difficult). When he went into lockdown mode, she was both attentive and compassionate. Clearly, there was something there.

She really stepped up in 2001, after Beau returned from postwar Kosovo, where he'd served as a legal advisor who helped train civil and criminal justice officials. He'd contracted a virus there that triggered ankylosing spondylitis, commonly known as bamboo spine, a horrific genetic disorder that causes bones in the back to freeze up, like acute arthritis. Beau was treated with Humira, then an experimental drug, at the National Institutes of Health (NIH) in Bethesda, Maryland. It proved effective, and Hallie tended to him throughout his treatment and recovery. They married a year after that.

At times, interactions between Hallie and Kathleen could get a little tense. Hallie confided to me that the night before their wedding, Beau told her, "Make it right. You need to because my brother means more to me than anything."

As couples—Hallie and Beau, Kathleen and me—we were together all the time. We spent every holiday together, every vacation together. Beau and Kathleen grew close. They laughed with each other all the time, a couple of practical jokesters for whom I was an easy target. Somewhere there's a photo of the two of them dangling a Thanksgiving turkey leg over my wide-open mouth as I lie sound asleep on a vacation-home couch. I loved it.

Hallie and I had none of that. We didn't have much in common, didn't even have much to talk about. She wasn't consumed by politics, wasn't devoted to the same issues that I was. But she's incredibly alluring—her wide eyes and flashing Cheshire cat smile are hypnotic. I could see why my brother fell for her. Hallie was proud of Beau and what they built as a family. That's what satisfied her in every way.

Beau's death tilted everyone's equilibrium in a manner I don't think any of us could have predicted. Life trajectories became entangled and dependent on others in whole new ways because of the outsized role Beau played in so many of our lives.

After the funeral, Hallie showed me a deep sense of compassion in making certain I took care of Beau's memory as he would've wished, most notably by helping her start the Beau Biden Foundation for the Protection of Children. She also allowed me to be there for Natalie and little Hunter, just as Beau wanted.

Our relationship started with me staying at Hallie's house to help with the kids. I fell right into the role. Driving the two hours between DC and Delaware, I'd get there in the early evening, in time for dinner or to take the kids to their soccer games. I'd then help put them to bed, often telling them stories about their dad; Natalie, especially, loved to hear tales about Beau and me growing up. I slept on a Murphy bed in the den, then took them to school in the morning before I headed back to Washington for work and my outpatient rehab. As time went on, we traveled as a pack to the movies, Sunday mass, the beach.

I was seduced by the idea of providing the same kind of extended family that surrounded Beau and me after we lost our mommy and sister, when Aunt Val lived with us and Uncle Jim converted our garage into an apartment. I'd even suggested to Kathleen after Beau's funeral that we move as a family into Hallie's Delaware house. That went nowhere.

My motivations were wrapped up in those kids. It all became about making sure I was there for them in the way I knew my brother would be there for my girls under the same circumstances. I knew in my bones what Natalie and Hunter were feeling because

I felt it, too. We had a unique relationship. I was part of raising my brother's kids before he died. I was a central person in their lives. It was the same relationship Beau had with my daughters. I never held back anything around Beau's kids, whether to counsel or reprimand them, and the same was true with him. My girls would talk with Beau about something that was bothering them as much as they would come to me, and Natalie and Hunter sought me out as much as they did their dad.

I didn't want to replace my brother. God knows I could never do that. But I did want to feel his presence. I did want to be reminded of him and thought that by being there with his children I could somehow resurrect that love.

Looking back, it's hard to tell if it was selflessness or selfishness on my part. I just don't know.

After Hallie and I returned from Sedona in the fall of 2016, our relationship remained a work in progress. We kept it to ourselves while we figured out where it might be headed.

That didn't last long. After our trip, Kathleen found texts between Hallie and me on an old iPad that I must have left at the house. That gave her the gift of justification: I was the sicko sleeping with my brother's wife.

Everything blew up after that.

On February 23, 2017, two months after Kathleen had filed for divorce, she filed a motion in DC Superior Court to freeze my assets. It was leaked to Page Six, the gossip sheet of the *New York*

Post. A week later, the news leaked that Hallie and I were dating. A *Post* reporter called to ask me to confirm or deny the relationship. It put me—us—in a box. A denial would make a lie out of what we were working on. A confirmation would unleash the tabloid world on our doorstep.

I opted for a straightforward affirmation. I said, honestly, that Hallie and I were "incredibly lucky to have found the love and support we have for each other in such a difficult time."

I asked my dad to make a statement, too, as a way to break it to the rest of our family. He'd left the vice president's office only a month earlier.

"Dad," I told him, "if people find out, but they think you're not approving of this, it makes it seem wrong. The kids have to know that there's nothing wrong with this, and the one person who can tell them that is you."

He was reluctant but finally said he'd do whatever I thought was best. His statement to the paper: "We are all lucky that Hunter and Hallie found each other as they were putting their lives together again after such sadness. They have mine and Jill's full and complete support and we are happy for them."

The story ran the next day, on March 1, under a headline that blared: BEAU BIDEN'S WIDOW HAVING AFFAIR WITH HIS MARRIED BROTHER.

It was the beginning of the end. Hallie was mortified. We became a tabloid drama narrated by the likes of the *Post*, TMZ, and the *Daily Mail*. Paparazzi tailed us nonstop. Our relationship wasn't just out in the open around Wilmington. It was on seventy-eight front pages around the world, from Thailand to the Czech Republic to Cincinnati.

Our lives of quiet desperation were suddenly on full display. I was madly trying to hold on to a slice of my brother, and I think Hallie was doing the same. Neither of us had yet thought of the relationship as a long-term or permanent commitment until it was made public, and then neither of us was prepared to let the other go. The spotlight forced us to make decisions we didn't want to make; if you've gone far enough to admit that you're in a relationship with your deceased brother's widow, or your deceased husband's brother, you'd better be all in. If we weren't all in, we worried, the relationship would be perceived as a salacious fling. So we tried to make something work that, in hindsight, was never in the cards.

Fallout rained down everywhere. My daughters were devastated. I lost nearly all of my clients and I had to resign from World Food Program USA. Almost everything I had business-wise or that was a passion of mine evaporated. Worse yet, I had started backsliding within months after returning from Sedona; had I been clean and sober, I might have dealt with all this more effectively. I might have prevented it from turning into something other than the dumpster fire it ultimately became.

Hallie and I didn't live together full-time until the end of that summer, when we moved to Annapolis. We wanted to get away from the fishbowl in Wilmington, while staying close enough for me to commute to Washington and to see my girls. It would be a fresh start. We rented a house and enrolled Natalie and Hunter in school there.

It was a bust right off the bat. I made it almost impossible for Hallie to get healthy as related to her grief and other issues she was dealing with, and she made it nearly impossible for me to do the same. It was a giant miscalculation on both our parts, errors in judgment born of a uniquely tragic time.

The truth is, neither of us could be trusted with making a proper cup of coffee, let alone making relationship choices while paparazzi jostled for a peek through our windows. We both were too enmeshed in our own problems to be capable of helping each other. As much as we desperately thought we could be the answers to each other's pain, we only caused each other more.

For Hallie, I was a constant reminder of what she once had and then lost. The life I was living was the antithesis of the life my brother had provided for her. I was in the throes of addiction. I was hardly present. I refused to be around when I was using because I didn't want to expose her and the kids to it, so I stayed away for long stretches. I kept making commitments to getting clean, and I would get clean, until I wasn't anymore.

For me, proximity to my brother's kids was at the top of the list of obligations I thought I owed to Beau. In reality, Natalie and Hunter needed their own time to heal, without being reminded of what wasn't there. As much as I could look and sound like Beau—as much physical and psychic DNA as we shared—I would never be able to replace their father. That was never my intent, of course, but it's also not the kind of thing that kids that young needed to be burdened with figuring out on their own.

Undoubtedly, my failures to get straight made everything harder. One thing every child needs is consistency, especially a child who has lost a beloved parent. Nothing in my life then provided for that.

Less than three months after we'd all moved in together, I essentially moved out. After a brief hiatus, during which I got sober, we tried it again in January. It was a new year—2018—and a clean slate. We rented a different house and enrolled the kids in school for another semester. It was hard for us to accept that we had misjudged things so badly, especially with all that Natalie and Hunter had already gone through.

That do-over lasted two weeks.

It felt like a failure of epic proportions. Our relationship had begun as a mutually desperate grasping for the love we both had lost, and its dissolution only deepened that tragedy. It made the obvious clear: What was gone was gone permanently. There was no putting Humpty Dumpty back together again.

That realization made it all the more difficult to pretend it could be otherwise, which made it all the more difficult for me to get clean. My oasis was gone.

What the fuck was I going to do now?

CHAPTER NINE

CALIFORNIA ODYSSEY

I used my superpower—finding crack anytime, anywhere—less than a day after landing at LAX in the spring of 2018.

I drove my rental to the Chateau Marmont, in West Hollywood, where I checked into a bungalow and by 4 a.m. had smoked every crumb of crack I'd brought. The clubs whose bouncers had served as my primary sources were closed, my calls to Curtis went unanswered, and my valet connection was AWOL.

I remembered a small crew of panhandlers who perpetually hung around a row of stores across from another club, near the corner of Sunset and La Brea, about a mile away. Like any worthy crack haunt by this point, it set off my spidey sense. When I pulled into the parking lot, there they were: a handful of guys loitering around a dumpster near the back. They'd improvised a small encampment of sleeping bags. They were clearly users.

I walked up and asked if they had anything that they'd sell. They did not and, at that hour, had no interest in looking elsewhere. Another guy from the group stepped out of the adjoining convenience store. He said he was sorry, that he didn't have anything, either, but he knew where to get some. He said we'd have to drive downtown.

He was about fifty and looked like he'd just gotten out of jail—in fact, he told me he'd been released that day. He kept pulling up his pants because he hadn't gotten a belt yet, and he carried everything he owned in a plastic CVS bag. That made him just desperate enough to get in a car with a stranger who easily could have been a cop.

I was just desperate enough to invite him in.

We hardly talked during the twenty-minute drive. He told me his name and that he'd served in the Air Force. Once we got downtown, past Pershing Square, he directed me through the deserted streets of the city's flower and fashion districts. Office and bodega storefronts were locked up tight. In the predawn darkness, a vast homeless enclave bloomed along the sidewalks on both sides of the street. Bunched together, block after block after block: pop-up tents, leaning cardboard boxes, tarps.

The scene looked postapocalyptic—or at least post–American Century. The area seemed darker than the rest of the city we'd just passed through, almost de-electrified, like the primitive dwellings that covered so much prime real estate. Trash littered the streets and the heavy, warm air stank of garbage and rot and sweat. Random shopping carts were piled high with a lifetime's worth of possessions; most of their owners were passed out nearby. The only cars I saw were police cruisers. We slid by at least three in the first few minutes after we arrived. A spooky silence added an even eerier atmosphere.

It was a dangerous place to visit and a more dangerous place to live. There was no brotherly, down-and-out kinship at that hour: when two people encountered each other, both froze and stared until somebody walked away—*if* somebody walked away. There was no "Hey, bro" conviviality. There was no testimonial to the human spirit underlying the nihilism.

There was no fucking poetry to it at all.

"Pull over here."

My guy got out with the $100 I gave him and told me not to stay parked on the street—too many cops. I watched him disappear through a cut between two tents, then circled the area. I was starting to get nervous after my third pass—conned again!—when I recognized my guy waving at me, a specter in the shadows. He got in the car with $100 worth of crack. I handed him another $200 and told him to use half of it for himself.

This time I only had to circle once.

The guy asked if I could drive him back to Sunset and La Brea. I dropped him off at the encampment there, then sped to my bungalow, the sun barely peeking over the horizon.

I returned to that scene by myself a few more times during my five-month self-exile in Los Angeles—a death wish, really. I'd head there after the clubs closed at four and the after-hours clubs closed at six and X, Y, or Z dealer had clocked out for the night. None of it would be up and running again until past noon. That was too long for me: I couldn't wait six hours for my next hit. The sun was up and I was still rolling, frenetic, jonesing.

Even in that crazed world, there's no master network available to someone who's up twenty-four hours a day, smoking every fifteen minutes, seven days a week. Nobody can attend to those needs. No matter how big a dispensation system somebody like me pieced together, there were always gaps in the service.

This downtown tent city filled in those gaps.

The first time I returned there alone I found the cut between the two tents that I'd watched my Air Force buddy slip through. As makeshift and chaotic as the layout seemed, there was a remarkable logic and consistency to it. I went through and stepped around people curled up on thin pieces of cardboard. Beyond them, I noticed a tilting, unlit tent. I pulled back a flap. It was pitch-black. All I saw was the gun pointed at my face.

I stood there unfazed: I assumed I was in the right place. If the guy squatting there had a gun, he had something worth protecting. Turned out I was right. I told him I'd been there before with Joe, or whatever name I gave him for the homeless guy who'd brought me there previously. His reply: "Who the fuck you talking about?" So I just asked if he had any hard. "Oh," he said. He lowered the gun, rummaged around, and pulled out a bag. He never even got up. I saw somebody else lying to his right, sound asleep, snoring softly. I only bought a little because he only had a little, but it was enough to hold me over until the rest of the miserable, bloodsucking world I now belonged to was up and back to work.

I walked straight to my car and slipped inside. I was shaking and ashamed. Then I lit up.

Thirty seconds later, I was numbed and flying and no longer ashamed at all—until the next time.

For months and months afterward—for most of the next year—there was always a next time.

It sounds absurd now, given that first day, but I came to California for a fresh start. I wanted a new place to be lost in and a certain level of anonymity. I wanted to get away from Washington and every bad reminder and influence there. I wanted to go someplace that wasn't always gray. I wanted a do-over. I planned to find a rental, settle in, and stay.

Instead, I holed up inside the Chateau for the first six weeks and learned how to cook crack. At that point in my free fall, I was acutely aware of the hotel's more depraved history. It was part of the attraction. My bungalow was near the one John Belushi died in from a drug overdose. Not long after Jim Morrison supposedly leaped from a fifth-floor window at the Chateau, he died in a Paris hotel bathtub. I thought about those kinds of things a lot. The amount of alcohol I consumed and crack I smoked was astounding—even death-defying. Morrison was a fucking piker compared to my shenanigans.

Cooking crack took practice, but it wasn't rocket science: baking soda, water, cocaine. That's it. I'd decided I wanted to cut out the middleman who could dilute the stuff with God knows what. Besides, my bungalow had everything I needed: stove, microwave, glass jars, and a tutor who made house calls—Honda, the skateboarder-turned-car-thief.

The most critical parts of the process are procuring a proper jar to cook it all in, one that's not too thin (it'll break) and not too thick (it won't heat properly); and getting the proportions just right. I became absurdly good at it—guess that 172 on my LSAT counted for something—though I wasn't beyond the occasional major fuckup. I'd heat the mixture over the stove in a baby food jar that would splinter and ruin everything. Or—this was later, in a hotel room without a stove or microwave—heat it with a torch lighter, hold the jar too long so it didn't cool down too quickly, and burn the shit out of my fingertips.

It's less potentially toxic to buy from somebody who knows how to cook. But cooking my own opened new avenues to me: there were ten times more people who sold powdered cocaine than sold crack. Buying it was a more genteel process, relatively speaking. Except for my desperate forays into Tent City, I figured I could eliminate one layer of drug-world repulsiveness.

I was off to the races.

With a room right by the pool, I didn't leave the Chateau's lush hillside grounds for a week or more at a time. I cooked and smoked, cooked and smoked. Occasionally, I slipped out late at night and drove for hours through the Hollywood Hills—back and forth on winding Mulholland Drive, up and down the switchbacking two-lane Laurel Canyon Boulevard. Even with LA's vast galaxy of lights twinkling below, it was like being dropped into a whole other world. It was wild and primordial and, except for the howl of a far-off coyote or some fierce avian screech, fantastically silent. I'd watch the sunrise from Runyon Canyon.

Subconsciously, it was the beginning of me falling in love with the California I love now, the one with untamed hollows and feral creatures tucked all around. Even in my ludicrous state, I kept those images in the back of my mind, noting that this could someday be a refuge. This was a place full of beautiful things, if only I could keep my eyes open long enough to appreciate them.

Sometimes I stopped and composed hurried letters about it to Beau:

Dear Beau,

It's different here than either of us thought it would be. It's not all just Beverly Hills on the beach. It's horse country and mountains. There's a real feeling of ancient wilderness that still exists here. You'd be amazed by the green of the city and how beautiful the Hollywood Hills are. Did you know there are mountain lions and coyotes here? I mean RIGHT HERE? I wish we'd both learned to surf. I remember when we used to say that you, me, and Dad were going to ride motorcycles up and down the Pacific Coast Highway. I regret we never did.

Love,

Hunter

Then I'd head back to West Hollywood to cook and smoke, cook and smoke.

The extent of my human contact was hanging out with a bunch of Samoan gangsters. I was connected to them through Curtis and his girlfriend.

For the next four or five months, my orbit was populated by an opaque, sinister night world of interconnected lives that roamed L.A. between 2 a.m. and 8 a.m. It mainly consisted of Curtis and his extended crew of thieves, junkies, petty dealers, over-the-hill strippers, con artists, and assorted hangers-on, who then invited their friends and associates and most recent hookups. They latched on to me and didn't let go, all with my approval.

I never slept. There was no clock. Day bled into night and night into day. With the curtains always closed, there was no visible distinction between the two. It got so disorienting at one point that I demanded one of the hangers-on pull open the shades so I could see for myself—see if it was day or night.

I came to dread sleep. If I rested too long between hits on a pipe, I'd be thrown into a panic. I'd crash for a few minutes, come to, and the first thing I'd demand would be "Where's the pipe?" Other times I'd reach for rocks that I'd left on a bedside table and then find, to my horror, that they'd been blown all over the room— somebody left a window or door open. I'd get down on my hands and knees to scan the floor and comb through the rug with my fingers. Half the time I had no idea what I was picking up: *Is this a flake of Parmesan from the cheese platter we ordered last night? Or crack?*

It didn't matter: I smoked it. If it was crack, great. If it wasn't, I'd take a hit, exhale, and exclaim: "Shit, that's not it—that's the fucking cheese!"

It got more pathetic. While driving around, I often snacked on white cheddar popcorn that I bought at convenience stores, eating it out of the bag. If I suddenly ran out of crack, I'd scrounge around my car's floor wells, cup holders, and door panels for any traces I might have dropped. Again, the crack crumbs were often indistinguishable from the spilled snacks. Safe to say I've smoked more cheddar popcorn than anybody on the face of the earth.

Over time, I trained my body to function on less and less sleep. After three days straight, I'd get droopy and zombie-walk everywhere. I'd push through it, though, and soon my body reset: I'd feel like I woke up at 8 a.m. after a weekend of lawn mowing and golf, ready for work. I'd smoke some more and be off to the races again for three more days, or six more days, or twelve more days.

My weekly sleep allotment usually topped out at about ten hours. Yet even that was irregular and mostly useless—definitely not REM sleep. I caught a few winks in my car while waiting on a dealer; on a toilet seat; on a chaise lounge by the hotel pool between hits. If I fell asleep there for too long, one of my room's misfit squatters was sure to shake me awake to cadge something new.

We've all been inside rooms we can't afford to die in. I put myself inside that room day after day, week after week, month after month.

I stayed in one place until I tired of it, or until it tired of me, and then moved on, my merry band of crooks, creeps, and outcasts soon to follow.

Availability drove some of the moves; impulsiveness drove others. A sample itinerary:

I left the Chateau the first time for an Airbnb in Malibu. When I couldn't reserve it for longer than a week, I returned to West Hollywood and the Jeremy hotel. There were then stays at the Sunset Tower, Sixty Beverly Hills, and the Hollywood Roosevelt. Then another Airbnb in Malibu and an Airbnb in the Hollywood Hills. Then back to the Chateau. Then the NoMad downtown, the Standard on Sunset. A return to the Sixty, a return to Malibu . . .

The scene was the same everywhere. I sometimes made sketches of the rooms' interiors but soon realized they all looked alike. I slapped a DO NOT DISTURB sign on the door first thing; a maid never entered. By the end of a stay, in the soft golden glow of the luxury room's light, the high-cotton-count bedsheets were strewn across the floor, plates and platters piled high from room service, the bedside phone knocked permanently off the hook.

An ant trail of dealers and their sidekicks rolled in and out, day and night. They pulled up in late-series Mercedes-Benzes, decked out in oversized Raiders or Lakers jerseys and flashing fake Rolexes. Their stripper girlfriends invited their girlfriends, who invited their boyfriends. They'd drink up the entire minibar, call room service for filet mignon and a bottle of Dom Pérignon. One of the women even ordered an additional filet for her purse-sized dog.

When they finished, two or three days later, they'd walk out with the hotel's monogrammed towels and throw pillows and comforters and ashtrays. Minimum-wage bouncers with side businesses—drugs, girls, access to VIP rooms for tips—now had a new hustle:

Me.

That's the business they were in. One night some women in my room started swapping stories they'd heard of a guy in the Hollywood Hills who'd created a social media platform, made millions if not billions, and now was addicted to drugs. They marveled at the stampede on his house to take his TVs and cars and the last dime in his bank account. They discussed it casually, almost professionally, like exchanging stock tips. Their takeaway: *I gotta get up there!* It was a way of life that revolved around feeding off people with money who have fallen into addiction.

I hardly held myself above them. I was just as much a part of the depravity as they were. I was smoking crack every fifteen minutes. They'd live off me until I said otherwise. As long as they didn't touch my drugs—or interfere with my ability to use, or create a scene that cut short my ability to stay at the hotel—I didn't give a damn.

Most of them came with their own drugs and focused on their own addictions: heroin, meth, drinking themselves to death. If I ran low on mine, I joined in with theirs. Misery really does love company.

I would get a room for one night. Then ask to keep it for another night. Then another. And another. When hotel management wanted me out, they'd refuse to extend my stay, politely but firmly telling me that someone else had reserved the room and there were no other vacancies. Other times the front desk informed me that guests were complaining about the parade of ne'er-do-wells traipsing in and out of my room and asked me to leave. I saw it as blatant racism and let them know it.

Once in a great while, some tender, desperate soul would float into the room who still seemed to possess a trace of kindness or concern. I'd wake up and find all my clothes folded and put back in the chest of drawers. I'd think, "Wow, she really is sweet." Then I'd find out she folded my clothes after going through all my pockets, taking everything and anything she could find. Others did the same thing with my bags or my car—just cleaned them out.

I lost count of the stolen wallets and credit cards. Charges rolled in: Gucci loafers, an $800 sport coat, Rimowa luggage. I'd trudge down to the Wells Fargo branch on Sunset to talk with one of the tellers about getting a replacement. They all knew me. They'd smile and send me to the same patient Armenian bank manager. Her usual first response: "We can't give you a new card without any ID."

But the more I came in, the more she took pity on me.

"Hunter," she would say with a sigh, "how can you keep losing your card all the time?"

The incongruity between the beauty I saw during my drives through the hills and the scummy subculture I willingly tapped into was demoralizing, depressing, defeating. It was so damn dark. I still feel a pit in my stomach when I think of how much money I dropped, how I allowed myself to think of any of those people as my friends. There wasn't a conversation that took place inside one of those hotel rooms in which anything genuine or enlightening was ever spoken. Not once. I wouldn't recognize 90 percent of them if we ran into each other again.

Yet I was so lost in my addiction that I watched the crowd rob me blind and didn't care enough to stop them—not as long as the cycle of drugs, sex, exhaustion, and exhilaration repeated itself over and over. It was nonstop depravity. I was living in some composite scene from *Fear and Loathing in Las Vegas* and *Permanent Midnight*, the adaptation of a TV writer's autobiography about his $6,000-a-week heroin habit, a movie that to this day makes me sick to watch because of its ugly parallels to my worst moments.

The self-loathing of that world only perpetuates itself. I wasn't without an understanding of the depravity of it. I was sickened by myself. It just kept going and going and going, and I couldn't figure out how to stop it. I was trapped in an endless loop and couldn't find my way out. I had removed myself from family, friends—everyone, really. I had removed myself from any restrictions.

It makes you hard in a way that's difficult to come back from. You're basically banishing your better self. Once you decide that you're the bad person everyone thinks you've become, it's hard to find the good guy you once were. Eventually, I quit looking for him: I decided I wasn't the person everybody who loved me thought I was anymore. So why continue to disappoint yourself? Why continue to disappoint them? Why not just disappear?

It's easier than you think.

I still held to my connection with Beau. Yet I felt even that slipping. As the summer wore on, the letters I wrote him in my journals began to sound more futile, more apologetic, less trusting in the notion that I'd ever find my way out.

Dear Beau,

Where are you? I'm here and you don't understand how bad it is. I know you're there but I need you. I know Dad is sick with worry about me but I don't know what to do about it. I'll figure this out, but I still need you. I can't stand that I can't touch you.

Love,

Hunter

And:

Dear Beau,

I promise you I'm trying with Natalie and Hunter. I probably screwed this all up but I don't know how to be here for them when I'm clearly not even here for myself. I feel like I've betrayed the one thing we never had to promise each other: to take care of each other's kids.

Love . . .

I never considered suicide, not seriously. But I did crave an escape, a reconnection—anything that wasn't this.

Dear Beau,

How do you expect me to be the one who's left behind? I don't know if I'm strong enough to do it. I don't seem to be doing any-

thing but causing more pain by sticking around. What would be
so bad about us being together?

Love . . .

I told family back in Delaware I was working on my sobriety—whatever the hell that meant at that point. Here's what it meant: nothing. I'd gotten good at telling stories like that.

It worked for a while. My girls would call; I'd tell them how much I missed them, that I'd see them soon, then hang up and cry for an hour. I'd do the same with Natalie and little Hunter. I'd end those calls feeling more alone and despondent and addicted than ever, with nowhere to turn and so turning away from everything, filling with self-pity—the addict's go-to reflex—and believing that they'd all be better off without me. How very fucking convenient.

Dad called, too, of course. I'd tell him everything was fine, all was well. But after a while, he wasn't buying it. My responses grew increasingly terse and intermittent. When I finally quit answering his calls altogether, along with my daughters', which only happened in the most extreme circumstances, he sent in the cavalry: my uncle Jim.

Uncle Jimmy is my best friend in the world and Dad knew that if his younger brother asked me to do something, I'd do it. Uncle Jim has his own superpower: he gets things done. So he jumped on a plane to Los Angeles, pulled me out of a room in the Hollywood Roosevelt, and said, "I found a place. Let's go."

I went. He checked me into a rehab center in Brentwood, where I stayed clean for about two weeks. I then lived in a rental off Nichols Canyon, in the Hills, with a sober coach. It was great—the beauty, the peace, the support—right up until the moment I relapsed.

My lesson after a spring and summer of nonstop debauchery: no lesson at all.

Just that it was awful.

Unimaginably awful.

CHAPTER TEN

LOST HIGHWAY

My penultimate odyssey through full-blown addiction became a shabbier, gloomier, more solitary version of the chromatic tear I went on through Southern California.

I came back east. The trees soon were bare and the low slate sky seemed to hover inches above my head. In my mind's eye, I can't picture a single day during my months back there that wasn't gray and overcast, a fitting, ominous backdrop.

I had returned that fall of 2018, after my most recent relapse in California, with the hope of getting clean through a new therapy and reconciling with Hallie.

Neither happened.

For all the obvious reasons—my extended disappearances, my inability to stay sober, her need to stabilize and reorder her own life and family—Hallie and I called it quits. The relationship no longer helped either of us. Our attempt to reanimate Beau remained as doomed as it was from the start. The fallout piled up. I tried to explain things to my daughters, but how could I expect them to comprehend a situation I hardly understood myself?

Next on my agenda was getting clean. I drove up to Newbury-port, Massachusetts, an old New England shipbuilding-turned-tourist town thirty-five miles north of Boston. A therapist ran a wellness center where he practiced a drug addiction therapy known as ketamine infusion. I would make two trips up there, staying for about six weeks on the first visit, returning to Maryland, then heading back for a couple weeks of follow-up in February of the new year.

After my many failed rehab attempts, I was certain that my getting clean depended on more than just being told addiction is a disease and that it requires 100 percent abstinence. While that works for many people, and at times has worked for me, I felt sure that underlying trauma was something that I needed to address, especially in the wake of Beau's death.

I'd done something similar in 2014 when I was treated in Mexico, with moderate success. That treatment—first using ibogaine, then 5-MeO-DMT, both psychoactive compounds—was mind-blowing in a very literal sense.

The ibogaine therapy was dark. After I ingested it alone in a quiet room inside the Tijuana clinic, a slideshow of my life had flickered before my eyes, one image-burst after another. I can't recall all of the visions, but I do remember having no control over them—that is, I couldn't stop them.

I also felt paralyzed, unable to move my arms, my legs, anything.

It scared the hell out of me; I worried I'd never move again. A nurse would come in to check on me, the creaking of the room's door screeching like nails on a chalkboard right next to my ear. Everything was heightened. That was followed by what they call a "gray day," a period when I felt as if I'd been in a deep depression. I slowly came out of it, and twelve hours after it began, the treatment was over.

I was taken from there to a beach house in Rosarito, a dozen miles south of Tijuana, to do 5-MeO-DMT therapy, which employs the gland secretions of the Sonoran Desert toad—that should give you an idea of the state I was in. A smart, gentle nurse assisted me through the whole thing, which lasted about thirty minutes, though it seemed more like three hours, or three days, or three years.

It was a profound experience. It connected me in a vividly renewed way to everyone in my life, living or dead. Any division between me, my dad, my mommy, Caspy, or Beau vanished, or at least became irrelevant. It felt as though I was seeing all of existence at once—and as one.

I know it sounds loopy. Yet whatever else it did or didn't do, the experience unlocked feelings and hurts I'd buried deep for too long. It served as a salve. I stayed sober for a year afterward—until I stormed out of that therapy debacle with Kathleen.

The ketamine sessions were equally intense, just as frightening, and not nearly as effective, though that's more on me than on them.

Originally developed as an animal tranquilizer and later used for surgical anesthesia during the Vietnam War, ketamine has become widely known for its illegitimate use as a club drug—Special K.

Medical researchers have found it to be effective in treating depression and post-traumatic stress disorder. As an extension of that, it has also been used to help break the cycle of drug dependence.

Its effect can be mind-bending and hallucinatory, though in a cogent, manageable way. You talk your way through whatever you're experiencing or seeing. For me, fears and past traumas surfaced vividly: Beau and me staying up late as kids, afraid that we'd wake in the morning to find Dad gone; the two of us looking at each other from hospital beds after the accident; the accident itself.

During and after those sessions, I longed even more for Beau's and Dad's presence, to feel their physical and psychic connection together, at the same time—the three of us as one again. I struggled to figure out how Dad and I fit together now, with such a large piece of the puzzle missing. I felt guilty and confused about that distance. I felt like I was killing off the one thing that could give me hope.

The therapy's results were disastrous. I was in no way ready to process the feelings it unloosed or prompted by reliving past physical and emotional traumas. So I backslid. I did exactly what I'd come to Massachusetts to stop doing. I'd stay clean for a week, break away from the center to meet a connection I found in Rhode Island, smoke up, then return. One thing I did remarkably well during that time was fool people about whether or not I was using. Between trips up there, I even bought clean urine from a dealer in New York to pass drug tests.

Of course, that made all that time and effort ineffective. I didn't necessarily blame the treatment: I doubt much good comes from doing ketamine while you're on crack.

The reality is, the trip to Massachusetts was merely another bullshit attempt to get well on my part. I knew that telling my family I was in rehab meant I could claim they wouldn't be able to contact me while I was undergoing treatment. I'd made my share of insincere rehab attempts before. It's impossible to get well, no matter what the therapy, unless you commit to it absolutely. The Alcoholics Anonymous "Big Book"—the substance abuse bible, written by group founder Bill Wilson—makes that clear: "Half measures availed us nothing."

By this point in my life, I'd written the book on half measures.

Finally, the therapist in Newburyport said there was little point in our continuing.

"Hunter," he told me, with all the exasperated, empathetic sincerity he could muster, "this is not working."

I headed back toward Delaware, in no shape to face anyone or anything. To ensure that I wouldn't have to do either, I took an exit at New Haven.

For the next three or four weeks, I lived in a series of low-budget, low-expectations motels up and down Interstate 95, between New Haven and Bridgeport. I exchanged L.A.'s $400-a-night bungalows and their endless parade of blingy degenerates for the underbelly of Connecticut's $59-a-night motel rooms and the dealers, hookers, and hard-core addicts—like me—who favored them.

I no longer had one foot in polite society and one foot out. I avoided polite society altogether. I hardly went anywhere now, except to buy. It was me and a crack pipe in a Super 8, not knowing which the fuck way was up. All my energy revolved around smoking drugs and making arrangements to buy drugs—feeding the beast. To facilitate it, I resurrected the same sleep schedule I'd kept in L.A.: never. There was hardly any mistaking me now for a so-called respectable citizen.

Crack is a great leveler.

Just like in California—like practically anywhere else I'd landed since this long bad dream began—each new day looked exactly like the one before it. Nothing occurred on a traditional wake-up/go-to-sleep continuum.

If I knew my crack connection, meaning if I'd bought from that person before and had his phone number, I would start making arrangements to buy from him as soon as I neared the end of my stash. If I reached him, I had to figure out how to meet with him. If we agreed on a time and a place, it was almost always at the most random hour, in the sketchiest part of town.

Impossible to factor into all of this: the waiting. No dealer works off a user's urgent timetable. So you arrange to meet in front of a 7-Eleven on such-and-such street, then sit in your car and wait. And wait. An hour passes since the time he said he'd be there. He doesn't answer his phone. You start freaking out. People keep going in and coming out of the store, and the man or woman working behind the counter keeps glancing your way, wondering why the hell you've been parked out there for two hours.

By this point, you're also about to jump out of your skin—you need that hit. You feel wholly depleted and it gets harder to keep your eyes open, even a little bit. You call the dealer's number a couple of times. Then a dozen times more.

You keep calling. He keeps not answering. The store clerk keeps staring.

Hours later, the dealer shows. No explanation. Odds are he has arrived with less than you asked for, or he wants more money than you've already agreed to pay. It's never straightforward. It's always some bullshit negotiation. You finally take what he has and hope it's what he says it is. Chances are better than even that the product is so trashed with look-alike filler as to have hardly been worth all the effort.

You're back on the phone three hours later, or eight hours later, cycling through the same routine two or three times more. By then, you no longer care or can tell whether it's morning or night. There's no longer any difference between 4 a.m. and 4 p.m.

It's so clearly an unsustainable life. The monotony is excruciating. It's truly the same thing over and over—same movies on TV, same songs on the iPod. Your mind is devoid of any thought other than how to get your next hit.

The motels where I stopped were frequented by active addicts who needed to support their addictions and pay their room bills. They ranged in age from their midtwenties to their forties and fifties. They were easy to spot. They stared out their windows or slouched outside their doors to see who might be a possible connection. Our rooms all faced one another, or they looked out onto a common parking lot. If you stared out your window long enough, you'd see who was going in and out of where, and who might have crack or information on where to find it.

Somebody would eventually come over to my room to sell me something directly, or pass along a connection, for a finder's fee. When we finished the transaction, the addict was usually out the door before I realized I was missing my watch or jacket or iPad— happened all the time.

More frustrating was when they told me they heard so-and-so had some good stuff, but he was in Stamford, about an hour away. I'd head to Stamford, wait in a parking lot there for an hour. A guy would finally show up with nothing, then make ten calls before tell-ing me about someone else with something in Bridgeport, a half-hour drive back up 95, where I'd have to wait another hour outside a bodega. Sometimes it paid off, sometimes it didn't. There were a million wild-goose chases.

One time I watched someone step into a room, close the door, then leave fifteen minutes later and head for his car. In a world filled with ex-felons carrying suspended licenses or no licenses at all and constantly bumming rides, this dude stood out. He was clean, barbered, and confident. But not cocky. He exuded . . . *ownership*. I caught up with him just before he pulled out and asked what I always asked: "Any hard?" Interactions like that were usually the beginning of one of two things: getting completely ripped off or a steady connection.

That's how I met John, who was the beginning of both.

John was a crack dealer from New Haven who'd already spent a decade in prison for dealing crack. In his mind, it was his only option. He said he had a family to feed. In a low, deliberate baritone, he told me stories about his life and kids. He engaged in discussions about world events. He was a rare thing in this particular universe: interesting. I ended up believing most of what he told me because I wanted to—because I had to.

John was never threatening, never even raised his voice. His power was far more debasing.

Much like Curtis in L.A., he was a master at feigned empathy. But Curtis worked in broad, easily detectable strokes that I just chose to ignore. Curtis wasn't a full-time dealer. As a wannabe music impresario and jack-of-all-trades hustler, he had other revenue streams. He could afford to show some humanity. He would sit me down and encourage me to get cleaned up. He knew I was killing myself, and he told me. But virtually in the same breath, he'd sell me more crack and keep the party going.

John was more of a miniaturist, a detail-oriented inveigler in the way he manipulated the human condition. Every gesture was purposeful, loaded, no matter how seemingly insignificant.

John would be considerate in small, symbolic ways that felt momentous in this hypertransactional setting. He'd pick up a sandwich and a bottle of orange juice from a convenience store for me before he came by to drop off some crack. "You have to eat, Hunter," he'd insist, spilling the contents of a bag onto my motel room bed. "You have to hydrate." He'd show up sometimes simply to check on how I was doing, see if I needed anything, make sure I was caring for myself.

Those minor acts of kindness were a seduction, of course, a kind of grooming. They were often followed by his insistence on the most trivial actions at the weirdest times. I'd be five dollars short on a $200 buy and he'd insist I go to an ATM immediately to get the cash—right after he'd bought me five dollars' worth of OJ and a ham sandwich at a mini-mart. Or he'd say that he'd given me more product than he was supposed to the day before, so now I owed him an extra $100. Or he wouldn't answer his phone for eight straight hours after he'd checked in on me and told me to call him anytime. As my frustration reached a breaking point, he'd call me back, say that he was on his way. He'd bring me a thermos of soup his wife made.

It was Drug Dealer 101, as seen on TV. Except I didn't have the option to dismiss him. He was a legit, reliable connection who allowed me mostly to avoid all the other knuckleheads out there who displayed many of the same deficits without any of his advantages.

He was most masterful at making me dependent on him. I was forced to adhere to his schedule, his whims. Once he had his hooks in me, he'd raise prices, make me jump through more hoops. I'd be waiting for him in a parking lot where he was already an hour late. He'd call to say he was pulling in now. He'd pull in four hours later.

He knew I wouldn't leave. Every move he made reinforced the power he held. He was humiliating, which was the point. The more he could humiliate me or any other customer, the more beholden we'd become. He had a steady source of income, and I had a steady if exasperating source of crack. It created a constant, back-and-forth tension: he was my jailer and my savior, both at the same time. I assume it's like Stockholm syndrome. There's an enormous amount of abuse you have to take as an addict, much of it by design. The abuse perpetuates the addiction by feeding the addict's sense of worthlessness, which swells the dealer's profit.

Still, after he'd shown up hours late and charged me way too much, I'd take a hit off the pipe and a sweet, welcome relief would wash all over me.

No one hooked me as mightily. No one played the game so mercilessly.

I felt trapped in my addiction's deepest, most hollowed-out hole yet. Alone in dim, mildewy motel rooms, unable to reach out or be reached, I sometimes called on the only emotional anchor I still possessed: the Hail Mary.

I repeated it over and over and over.

I was raised Catholic and worked for the Jesuits, but the prayer's effectiveness for me in times of distress is not tied to a deep-seated belief in the Church. At least not directly. While it's a prayer every Catholic kid memorizes in the first grade, I learned it far earlier. It was the prayer my grandmother recited to me and Beau when she came into our bedroom at night to put us to sleep. She'd lie with us and scratch our backs while she told us stories about our mommy and what a wonderful and amazing human being she was. When she saw that our eyelids were heavy and about to shut, she would recite, aloud, three Hail Marys and one Our Father.

When she finished and left our room, Beau would call out to me from his bed, "Good night, bud. See you in the morning," and I'd have to call back, "Okay." If I called out anything else, or if I just kept quiet—which I sometimes did, just to mess with him in a little-brother sort of way—Beau would stay up and pester me until I said it. For Beau, it was an obsessive, superstitious ritual: as long as he said, "Good night, bud," and I answered, "Okay," he believed that nothing could stop us from waking up to each other in the morning.

I reenacted that send-off with myself many nights inside those sad little motel rooms dotted along I-95. With the muted rumble of semis barreling down the nearby highway and the inane chatter and cackles of other residents drifting through my door from the parking lot, I'd call out aloud, in the dark, "Good night, buddy. See you in the morning."

There was no response, of course, which only made Beau's absence more acute. Sometimes I woke in a panic because the nightmare my brother worried so much about had come true: nobody had responded "okay," and now Beau really, truly, undeniably wasn't there.

So I'd chant the Hail Mary, like a mantra, like a hymn. Sometimes I went on for what seemed like hours. I couldn't fall asleep, and I couldn't stop repeating it. If I did, the pain of Beau's distance came flooding back.

Hail Mary, full of grace,
The Lord is with thee . . .

One day, out of the blue, three or four weeks into this madness, my mother called.

She said that she was having a family dinner at the house, that I should come, even stay in Delaware for a few days. It would be great; we hadn't had everyone together in ages. I was in lousy shape but it sounded appealing. I pulled out of a motel parking lot, said goodbye to all that, and headed to Wilmington.

I believe I arrived on a Friday night. I walked into the house, bright and homey as always, and immediately saw my three daughters. I knew then that something was up: Naomi had come in from New York, where she was in law school at Columbia; Finnegan came in from Philadelphia, where she was at Penn; and Maisy, then a high school senior, had come over from Kathleen's house, in Washington. I then saw my mom and dad, smiling awkwardly, looking pained.

A moment later, I spotted two counselors from a rehab center that I'd once gone to in Pennsylvania. That was it.

"Not a chance," I said.

My dad suddenly looked terrified.

"I don't know what else to do," he cried out. "I'm so scared. Tell me what to do."

My flat reply:

"Not fucking this."

It was awful.

I was awful.

It devolved from there into a charged, agonized debacle. I refused to sit down with the counselors, refused to sit with my dad. Everybody was crying, which only made me angrier.

"Don't ever ambush me like this again," I told my dad, and bolted out of the house.

He chased me down the driveway. He grabbed me, swung me around, and hugged me. He held me tight in the dark and cried for the longest time. Everybody was outside now. When I tried to get in my car, one of my girls took the keys and screamed, "Dad, you can't go!" I shouted back at her, "You're not doing this!" I lashed out at my mother for deceiving me. I lashed out at I don't know who else. It was a raw, appalling experience for all of them.

To end it, I agreed to check into a rehab center, though not the one that the two counselors there had come from. I made up some excuse. It was nonsense; I always had a million excuses. Dad pleaded with me, "Anything. Please!" I could be suitably functional in high-pressure situations like that. I finally said I would go to another center nearby, in Maryland. Somebody immediately called to make arrangements.

Hallie picked me up late that night and drove me the thirty miles to the center. We were done, but I guess we had that much left. We argued the whole way until we fell silent. When we got to the rehab center, I had her drop me off at the front gate. I walked through the lobby doors and, as soon as I saw her drive off, called an Uber. I told the staff there that I'd return in the morning, then caught my ride and checked into a hotel in Beltsville, Maryland, near the Baltimore/Washington International Airport.

For the next two days, while everybody who'd been at my parents' house thought I was safe and sound at the center, I sat in my room and smoked the crack I'd tucked away in my traveling bag.

I then boarded a plane for California and ran and ran and ran.

Until I met Melissa.

CHAPTER ELEVEN

SAVED

By the time my plane touched down in Los Angeles in March 2019, I had no plan beyond the moment-to-moment demands of the crack pipe.

I was committed to one thing: vanishing for good. That was my lone, next-level goal. No matter how low I'd been before, a voice deep inside had always fought to pull me out of my nosedive. It's why I'd allowed my uncle Jimmy to haul me from a West Hollywood hotel room months earlier and escort me to a rehab center. That turned out to be an unsuccessful three-week stab at sobriety, but it still left me with a glimmer of hope and striving to climb out of my ditch. It's why I sought out something as fraught and audacious as ketamine therapy when I drove up to cold, gray Massachusetts that winter, as botched and pathetic as the attempt turned out to be.

I would take one step forward and ten steps back—but I was still taking steps. I didn't want to drown in addiction's quicksand. I did not want those attempts to fail.

I just couldn't make them work.

I longed for a connection with someone outside of addiction's airless bubble—someone with whom I had no past, no baggage, and to whom I owed neither explanations nor apologies. I wanted to have conversations with someone who wasn't a dealer or gangbanger or bouncer or stripper. Three years earlier, even as I'd craved those hotel mini-bottles of vodka in Amman, I could still sit across from the king of Jordan and discuss the plight of Syrian refugees, Middle East dynamics, and the existential obligations of being a great man's son. I thought then that maybe that was my addiction's low point— I thought that was the sound of me hitting bottom.

Back then, I still hoped to paint again, still hoped my journal entries could someday turn into a book, still dreamed of hugging my daughters tight every day. If I could find some new treatment, some new approach, some new . . . *lifeline*, I thought I could still claw my way back out.

During the nearly four years of active addiction that preceded this trip to California, which included a half dozen rehab attempts, that's what I told myself after each failure. As bad as it got, I believed what Beau had believed: good or bad, it was all part of the process.

Stepping off the plane this time at LAX, however, it was clear that all of the options I once clung to were now pipe dreams. I consciously stopped even pretending I would get better. I dove headfirst into the void.

It's hard to describe just how paralyzed and hopeless you can become in your addiction, how you can reach depths you never thought possible, and then drop even further—in this case, uncomprehendingly further. This period felt more dangerous, more fatally alluring, than any time before. I surrendered completely to my grimmest impulses. I was like someone picking out a firearm in a pawn shop, fully aware I was choosing a certain kind of death.

Disappearing was the only thing that gave me solace. It meant an end to pain. It meant I didn't need to think about how much I was disappointing my brother, even though I knew Beau would never think of it that way. I quit writing him letters, feeling as if I didn't have anything authentic to communicate to him anymore. Disappearing meant freedom from feeling. Thinking that you have something to live for obligates you to muster the courage and energy to fight.

I didn't want to fight.

I finally silenced the dialogue that I'd kept up inside my head about getting clean and rebuilding my life. It was ridiculously easy: I just drowned it out with more and more drugs. Now I never thought, as I always had at some point in the midst of my previous binges, *I'm just going to do this until . . .* I no longer said *until*. I no longer finished the sentence. I gave up on everything. I stopped trying to fool others into thinking I was okay. I stopped trying to fool myself.

I was done with finding my way back into the world I had known my whole life. I was done trying to figure out how to return to a law firm. Done with the world of politics, of figuring out how to go out on the campaign trail with Dad, if it came to that, as I would have in any other election year. Done coming up with excuses for why I lived where I was living and why I did what I was doing.

I was a crack addict and that was that.

Fuck it.

My first call off the plane was to a drug connection.

I took an Uber to my car, which I'd stored in the garage of someone who managed a place I had stayed at. (Side note: this being an L.A. friend at that time, he had tried to sell the car.) I went straight from there to pick up some crack.

The next month and a half is a drug-befuddled blur. That's not a dodge or a lapse in memory. Everything that followed my return to L.A. was a genuine, dictionary-definition blur of complete and utter debauchery. I was doing nothing but drinking and drugging.

I spent the first couple of weeks at an Airbnb in Malibu. It was around then that Rudy Giuliani began his ad hominem attacks against me, in anticipation of my father's run for president. They centered on my work for Burisma, with dubious details collected from his "interviews"—that is, drunken lunches and dinners—with former Ukrainian prosecutors Viktor Shokin and Yuri Lutsenko, both of whom have been subjects of corruption accusations.

The smears came out of the blue, without warning. No one ever called to say, "Get ready for this, Hunter." The first time I became aware of it was while browsing the Apple News feed on my iPhone.

I didn't know what the hell to make of it. I watched a video in which Giuliani looked beyond unhinged. He appeared to be drunk but almost intentionally so, as if it were part of a choreography designed to better rile his boss's appreciative base. His accusations and insinuations were so outlandish, so outside of any reality, that it actually struck me that he was doing a disservice to himself. I couldn't see how any of it would become an issue, even after Trump started weighing in.

Breitbart and the rest of the right-wing crowd swiftly jumped on board and trotted out their familiar suite of distortions. They pounded me not only for my connection to Burisma but also for my work as a lobbyist and my first job out of law school, in Delaware. They questioned how I got fast-tracked in MBNA's executive management program, failing to mention I was a Yale Law grad with my pick of opportunities.

Those attacks prompted more mainstream news outlets to run stories that countered the distortions with actual reporting. Yet in doing so, in the name of objective journalism, each story repeated the attacks made against me. It became a predictable cycle in a media ecosystem that manages to spread falsehoods even as it debunks them. Trump and Giuliani understand that system as only mad scientists can.

It drove me deeper into my hole, made me more certain there wasn't a way back. I quit responding to the constant calls from Dad and my girls, picking up just often enough to let them know I was alive and seeking help, which in turn gave me cover to burrow back into oblivion.

It was around this time that Adam Entous, a Pulitzer Prize–winning writer at the *New Yorker* magazine, emailed me an interview request for a story he was writing about Burisma and how my work there squared with Dad's anticorruption actions in Ukraine. He said he simply wanted to get to the bottom of the allegations.

I had been obsessed with the magazine when I was younger and had other aspirations. I devoured every issue—the poetry, the fiction, all of it. I thought the pinnacle for a writer was to be published in the *New Yorker*, the *Paris Review*, or *Poetry* magazine. It wasn't snobbery. It was respect. That's why I called Adam back, even though I didn't know him personally. We soon began to talk by phone almost every night for the next several weeks.

What started out as conversations about my business dealings, which we covered extensively, soon turned into a personal tell-all. From Adam's perspective, the story was an attempt to understand my role with a Ukrainian energy company. For me, it was an opportunity not only to give my side of that story but to shout to the world, "Here I am!"—an emphatic counterweight to "Where's Hunter?" I decided I wasn't going to hide who I was anymore. You want to know about my life? Here are the gory details.

Fuck it.

So I talked. And talked. Each night, wherever I happened to be staying, I propped my cell on a desk or table in front of me or positioned it on my chest while I lay in a hotel bed, set it to speaker, and answered any question Adam asked from his home office in Washington, where he would call from after helping put his kids to bed.

I didn't tell him I was actively smoking crack at the time. Shortly after the interview sessions began, the noise from Giuliani died down for a bit and I moved to the Petit Ermitage, a discreet, ivy-cloaked boutique hotel tucked away on a quiet block between the raucousness of Sunset and Santa Monica Boulevards in West Hollywood. I'd driven past it one day on my way somewhere else, was struck by its mysterious, half-hidden charm, and checked in.

I didn't notify my dad or his campaign about the *New Yorker* story. I didn't want input from the communications team. They were only weeks away from publicly announcing, via a video released on the morning of April 25, that Joe Biden was running for president in 2020—joining the battle, as my dad put it, for "the soul of the nation." I knew damn well how they would react to my story, which would be published in early July, just after the primary's first debate: they'd flip out and do everything they could to quash it.

I knew what the story would really do: inoculate everybody else from my personal failings. I wanted to make it so there couldn't be anything held over my dad's head. There would be no opposition press coming to the campaign saying, "We're about to run a story on Hunter being a crack addict," making everybody scramble to figure out what to do next.

I was taking that problem off the table. Besides, nobody was going to vote or not vote for my dad because his son is a crack addict. Hell, even Trump knew that.

I knew exactly what I was doing. I knew that our family was going to be attacked, and our lives turned upside down, no matter what. If political enemies didn't come after me, they'd mug somebody else in the family. The only question my dad had to consider in deciding whether or not to run for president was the same one he dealt with in 2016: Is it worth it?

He knows everyone in our family believes it's worth it. Nobody said to him, "Joe, please don't do this; they're going to murder me."

It's not in our vocabulary, not how we size up any political land-scape. He knew I was in the midst of a personal slide. Yet the confidence my father has in me is evidenced by the fact that he still ran.

What I didn't count on when I agreed to talk for the *New Yorker* story, at least at first, was how cathartic the experience would be. The conversations became like nightly therapy sessions. I talked to Adam about Beau and Dad and how much they meant to me, about my personal and professional choices, about my alcoholism and drug addiction. I opened up about all of it with an honesty I hadn't talked with to anyone else except a therapist, a fellow addict in recovery, or my family. I told him the truth about how I got to where I was.

Subconsciously, the process kept me tethered to the only constant sources of love since the day I was born: my brother and my dad. I didn't realize it at the time, but explaining those relationships was the one thing that kept my eyes open wide enough to recognize salvation when it eventually presented itself: I honestly believe I would not have been capable of seeing Melissa for what she would become to me if I hadn't explored my most meaningful relationships during those interviews. It was a little miracle.

The other twenty-two hours of my day, however, were spent doing every miserable thing I could to bury it all in a deluge of crack and booze. As personal as it was, what made coming clean to the *New Yorker* a relatively easy exercise was the fact that I thought I was doing it for the last time. I wasn't clearing a path for reentry into the mainstream. I believed the story would expedite my fade-out—that after exposing myself for who I really was, without embarrassment or regret, I would no longer be welcome back in the world I'd left behind. It was my opportunity to tell everyone out there, *"This is who I am, you motherfuckers, and I ain't changing!"*

I picked up where I left off during my last rampage through L.A., except now I was far less concerned with how I interacted with the "normal" world. By this point, that world was largely confined to the hotel management and staff at the Petit Ermitage. The usual parade of dealers and their hangers-on streamed in and out of my room at all hours, without any attempt by me or them to be the least bit prudent. We stuck out like sore thumbs; even in L.A., where everyone poses like a tough guy, I had guests visit at 4 a.m. who looked like they'd just stepped out of a Quentin Tarantino movie. Sometimes I stashed my drug paraphernalia when a housekeeper came by; sometimes I didn't. My belongings were strewn everywhere, along with pipes and baggies and baking soda, which I used whenever I cooked my own.

My $300-a-night room looked like somebody set off a bomb in a crack house.

As I always did, I rented the room a day at a time, unwilling or incapable of planning any further ahead than that. I'd call the front desk each morning to ask for another night's extension. The routine was disrupted about two weeks into my stay when Curtis came by the rooftop pool one night for drinks. He got loaded and almost wound up in a fight with a big, swaggering drunk who earlier had been acting like a complete asshole—he'd jumped a line to the hotel's unisex bathroom.

Later that night, when Curtis and I stepped into the hotel's elevator to leave the fourth-floor pool area, the jackass he'd almost scuffled with earlier got on board, too. Curtis practically bored a hole through the dude with his most menacing glare—which, believe me, is pretty damn menacing. We all left the elevator without incident, but the guy later told security Curtis had threatened him during the ride by giving him a peek at his gun.

A hotel manager called my room the next morning. He said someone had reported that a guest of mine had threatened to kill him. I explained that the whole thing was blown out of proportion and had been resolved. When I made my usual call to the front desk a little later to re-up for another night, however, I was told my room had been booked in advance for the next week and there was nothing else available.

I was used to this; it happened all the time. I was the guy by the pool who got up every ten minutes to duck into the bathroom and smoke crack. I was the guy who sat by himself at the bar and piled up a $400 tab without buying drinks for anyone else. The staff must've thought, *How is that guy still standing?*

As much as I thought I was in control, I wasn't fooling anybody. Four or five days into a stay, I'd call the desk to reserve another night and be told there were no more rooms at the inn. Everyone was polite; they were always well-mannered. No one ever formally threw me out—though the Chateau eventually blacklisted me, putting me on their infamous unofficial rogue's lineup that included the likes of Britney Spears, if that gives you an idea of how out of control I was.

Now, the Petit Ermitage asked me to vacate my room by 11 a.m.

There was no way I could pack up my wreckage by then, and I had no idea where to go next. I missed the morning deadline and had it extended to 1 p.m., then to 3. In the meantime, I settled into a shaded lounge chair by the rooftop pool and tried to pin down my next move. I slipped away every twenty minutes to hit the crack pipe in my room, on the same floor just down the hall. I finally got a bellman to help me round up my belongings and hold them for me in the lobby.

At one point, a young, trim, artsy guy in a chaise lounge next to mine struck up a conversation. He'd done the same thing the day before, even though I'd made it clear I didn't really want to talk with anyone. It was a tight-knit, very L.A. scene up there that I wanted nothing to do with—I hadn't made new friends in three years unless they were involved with drugs.

But here he was again, yakking away. This time he was with a tall, blond Daryl Hannah look-alike and a photographer friend. He'd obviously had too many drinks. "Here's the most interesting person at the pool," he greeted me as he sat down this time. "What's your story?" He then proceeded to tell me his: all about his burgeoning career as a painter and sculptor. I nodded once in a while: I'd probably already drunk a quart of vodka that day, smoked crack continuously, and was operating on ten hours of sleep for the week.

I don't know how long he went on. The only thing I remember is that all of a sudden one of the trio turned to another and said, "You know who Hunter should meet? He should meet your friend Melissa."

They agreed right away and insisted I take Melissa's number. I didn't write it down; I told them I had a gift for memorizing phone numbers. Some friends of theirs came by after that and they left me alone. I continued to search my phone for another place to stay the night. When I finally got up to leave, the Daryl Hannah look-alike turned to me and asked me to repeat Melissa's number. At that point, I could hardly remember my own name. She smiled as she pulled a pen from her purse and scribbled Melissa's contact on my hand.

An hour or so later I checked into the Sunset Marquis, a half mile away, and resumed my drinking and drugging. Sometime after midnight I noticed the number inked across my palm and texted someone named Melissa to see if she wanted to meet for a drink. I'm sure I had no good on my mind. Melissa's response was swift, polite, and to the point: "No thank you. I'm asleep."

I shuffled into the shower and scrubbed the number off my hand. My crackhead brain sure as hell didn't memorize it. I toweled off and reached for a pipe.

If this were a more probable story—if this were a movie that followed my narrative arc to its more plausibly tragic outcome—my future would have ended there.

It would've run off my hand with Melissa's phone number and slid down the drain for good.

Instead, Melissa texted me in the morning. She asked if I wanted to meet for coffee; her friends had encouraged her to do so. I texted back that I could meet her at eleven at the restaurant inside the Sunset Marquis. I waited at a table there until she texted again to say she was running late and could we meet instead at one. A little later, she asked if we could make it four.

Remarkably, I wasn't already totally fucked-up; for reasons I still can't decipher, I hardly smoked or drank at all that day, unlike every other day since I'd returned to Los Angeles. For one thing, I hadn't shared my latest whereabouts with my traveling band of vampires. So my only human contact that day was with an actual civilian: Melissa. Yet when five o'clock rolled around, I assumed she'd blow me off again, and sure enough, she texted an apology for canceling so many times, then promised she would be there, for dinner now, at 5:15.

I made my way to the dining room, not really clear why anymore, other than that I'd gotten myself into this mess and figured I'd let it run its disastrous course. That had been my MO for most of the last four years anyway. Still, I had showered and pulled on a pair of jeans and a denim jacket—what Beau and I used to call a Canadian tuxedo. It was my first actual date in twenty-six years. My relationship with Hallie belonged to a whole other category, and the other women I'd been with during rampages since my divorce were hardly the dating type. We would satisfy our immediate needs and little else. I'm not proud of it. It's why I would later challenge in court the woman from Arkansas who had a baby in 2018 and claimed the child was mine—I had no recollection of our encounter. That's how little connection I had with anyone. I was a mess, but a mess I've taken responsibility for.

Not that I was sure that this coffee-turned-lunch-turned-dinner with Melissa was going to head anywhere. I didn't want a relationship, certainly nothing with strings attached. I just wanted to be gone.

As I stepped past the restaurant's outdoor seating area, set in a kind of lush secret garden, I spotted a woman seated alone at a table. Lit by the glow of L.A.'s gauzy spring light, with oversized sunglasses pushed atop her honey-blond hair to reveal the biggest, bluest eyes I'd ever seen, the woman I took to be Melissa glanced my way and flashed a bright, easy smile. It floored me. It was full of warmth and free of guile. A charge rushed through my body—the first genuine, non-crack-aided jolt to my system that I'd experienced since I could remember. It was electrifying.

It was a bell ringer.

My boots clacked under me as I continued on to the restaurant's front entrance and navigated my way to the table. Tiny white lights were strung through trees that ringed a terraced wall. We both smiled as I sat down.

I spoke up first.

"You have the exact same eyes as my brother."

Then, not long after that, having no idea what I was going to say until it jumped out of my mouth:

"I know this probably isn't a good way to start a first date, but I'm in love with you."

Melissa laughed. Again, it was electric. When a waiter came by to take a drink order, I told him Melissa probably needed something strong "because I just told her I'm in love." The three of us laughed aloud together.

An hour later, Melissa said she was in love with me.

An hour after that, I told her I was a crack addict.

"Well," she responded to that news, without blinking or hesitating, "not anymore. You're finished with that."

My reaction:

"Okay."

I had no idea what I meant. There's a point you reach in addiction—a point I had so clearly reached—where you believe it's impossible to ever be in a healthy, life-affirming relationship again. You've accrued too many deficits. When you tell a person who you really are—in my case: crack addict—you scare them to fucking death. They rightly become protective of their own hearts, their own sanity, no matter what they might think of you otherwise. With me, you could also toss in a messy divorce, a very public affair, and the daily grenades lobbed my way from the White House. Googling me was enough to send anybody running.

Yet, in an instant, I knew this: I was finished with what I'd come to California to start. I went from completely giving up on the notion of ever trying again—trying to get clean, trying at life—to knowing I was finished with whatever kept me from trying both those things. Here was a magnificently beautiful woman sitting across from me, dressed casually in a light blue denim blouse and jeans, speaking in the noblest South African accent, who was so fearless that she didn't head for the hills the moment I said I was madly in love with her—and then that I was a crack addict. I was all in.

I realize how crazy that sounds. But I was 100 percent sure of it; there were no butterflies in my stomach, only the certainty that this could be my last chance. For me, having the confidence to express that I wanted to spend the rest of my life with someone as well as confess my addiction was my way of saying, "You're going to have to help me with that last one." I wasn't surprised in the least that Melissa didn't balk. I saw something in her eyes the moment I looked into them: everything was going to be okay.

Crack addict, alcoholic, tabloid mainstay, political punching bag—it all had become such a profound part of who I was that it made it seem impossible I'd ever find somebody willing to work past any of those things.

Yet Melissa didn't flinch. She didn't turn away in shock or disgust. I told her about my addiction and my alcoholism. I told her about my divorce and about Hallie. I told her about my brother, my mother, my baby sister, my grief. I told her about my pain, about what they refer to in AA as the "God-sized hole" inside me. I rolled out an unvarnished version of the last four years and beyond.

Melissa absorbed it all. There was no stigma to addiction for her. She had known and loved too many friends and acquaintances who'd battled it, and she was committed to staying in the battle with me. She saw addiction as something the soul had to work through and be done with before one could move on to the next great thing. Setbacks weren't world-ending. She put a karmic topspin on Beau's part-of-the-process approach, but they amounted to the same thing. I felt in strong and steady hands.

Melissa then unreeled her story. She was a thirty-two-year-old activist proficient in five languages ranging from Italian to Hebrew and an aspiring documentary filmmaker who had spent time living with and filming indigenous African tribes. As a toddler she was placed in a children's home for a year before being adopted by a South African family with three boys, in Johannesburg. She had come to the U.S. to visit friends in L.A. during a gap year after attending the University of Johannesburg, intending to go on to India, but stayed when she fell in love and got married. It didn't last long. A two-year live-in relationship had ended just a few weeks before.

In fact, Melissa explained that she'd canceled on me so many times that day because she'd just flown back from visiting one of her brothers, who now lived in Atlanta. He'd consoled her over the breakup of that relationship, which she knew she should've exited much earlier. I later learned she'd told me things that night that she'd never talked about with anyone.

We hardly noticed the waiter whenever he came by; I guess we ate and drank. Two hours in we were discussing the kind of life each of us wanted. Before long, we mused about the kind of life we could have together. We both agreed we wanted to stay in California. When I told her about my three daughters, she said she'd love to have children someday. Not long after that, we talked about the possibility of that being something we could do together.

It went on like that for more than three hours. It was intense, raw, utterly bewitching. Melissa later said she felt as if she'd met a friend she'd known her whole life, but whom she'd been separated from for years and was finally getting to see again. I felt completely at ease, wide-open, mesmerized.

By the time we left, the tree lights strung around us twinkled in the gathering dusk. The scene had turned magical. I drove Melissa to meet up with a friend at the Chateau Marmont—thank God all

I got was a smirk and a nod from one of the valets—and we went from there to a birthday party for another friend of Melissa's at a nearby Mexican restaurant. Everyone was gathered around one big table. Amid all the unfamiliar faces, I felt a familiar twitch. I'd been so enraptured during dinner that I hadn't hit the pipe all night. It was the longest I'd intentionally gone without using since I'd landed back in L.A. Now, before sitting down, I told Melissa I was going to run out to get a birthday gift, and assured her I'd be right back.

I drove to the hotel and headed up to my room. Before locating my pipe, I settled into a chair near the window, took a deep, reflective breath, and closed my eyes for just a moment, pausing to absorb everything that had happened that evening. When I opened them again, it was 7:15 a.m.

I panicked. I thought I'd blown my one chance at salvation. I fumbled around for my phone and saw a text Melissa had sent sometime after I left the restaurant the night before.

"Is everything okay?"

I texted back immediately to say how sorry I was. I told her I'd returned to my room exhausted and fell asleep. I promised it was an honest mistake.

Fifteen long minutes later, Melissa replied.

"Glad you're okay. What are you up to today?"

"Spending time with you?" I typed hopefully.

Melissa asked if I wanted to come by her apartment and go from there to get breakfast. I raced over and apologized fifty times for flaking out the night before. She insisted it was no problem. We sat for a minute on the couch inside her modest one-bedroom in a pink stucco complex just up the street from the Petit Ermitage, whose verdant rooftop pool was visible from the fourth-floor walkway outside her front door. I lowered my head into her lap, then didn't wake up until that night. Opening my eyes and seeing that she was still there, I remember telling her, with utter relief and without equivocation or exaggeration, "That's the first time I've slept in three years."

From that day on, Melissa nursed me back to health.

Nursed me back to life.

The first thing she did: took my phone, my computer, my car keys. She took my wallet. She deleted every contact in my cell that wasn't my mom, dad, aunt, or uncle—anybody whose name didn't contain Biden. Gangbangers, bouncers, valets—all gone. If you weren't blood, you were out. When I protested that lifelong friends were getting erased in the massacre, Melissa calmly countered that they'd find a way to reach me if they were truly lifelong friends. She reset the password on my laptop and didn't tell me what it was, ensuring that I had to go through her to use it.

She dumped out all of my crack. I couldn't go to the bathroom without her following me inside, sure that I'd hidden something in there. I had. I'd wake up in the middle of the night and she'd tail me into the living room. I'd insist I was fine, that I just couldn't fall asleep, hoping that she'd head back to bed. I only wanted a minute to rifle through my bags for whatever residual dope I could find. I didn't realize she'd already gone through every bag I owned and tossed out anything that resembled a drug, from Advil to my unused Lexapro.

The vultures didn't wait long to call and knock. Their cash cow was missing, and they wanted me back. They said I owed them money and tried to intimidate Melissa if I didn't pay up. She turned to steel. She was merciless. She went through my bank records and checked off charges, like the $15,000 worth of purchases at a Best Buy in the Valley, where one of my dealers lived. She then told my former compatriots in debauchery in no uncertain terms that if they showed up at her door or tried to get in touch with me again she was calling the police and would otherwise turn their futures into a living hell. The South African beauty with the bottomless blue eyes made that crystal fucking clear. She changed my number and within weeks would find a house for us tucked high in the Hollywood Hills. She pushed away everyone in my life connected to drugs.

It was all on Melissa. It's no picnic trying to monitor and manage an addict. It's an enormous amount of work. It's onerous and frightening. Nobody wants to be anyone's jailer, and Melissa was imprisoned as much as she felt she needed to temporarily imprison me. She had to put up with my whining and crying and scheming. I tried to negotiate an agreement for a slow weaning process off crack. She said no—*hell no*—though she did ease me off drinking by first allowing three drinks a day, then one drink, then nothing, while also arranging for a doctor to come to the apartment and administer an IV to remedy any nutritional deficiencies and aid with my withdrawal.

When I tried to sneak around, she busted me. I tried to convince her through sheer force of personality that it wasn't fair to make me stop using crack all of a sudden—that it was, in fact, dangerous.

She called bullshit.

I never ran, never resented her taking that kind of control. I knew she was saving my life. I was certain that if I had my keys and wallet and phone for two hours while she went out grocery shopping, I would relapse. The gratitude I felt only deepened the connection that was already deeper than anything I could imagine. I'm certain there was no one else in my life capable of doing what Melissa was doing, though not for lack of effort or love. At that moment, I required the impossible: a foreign body with a familiar soul.

That was Melissa.

When it sank in for me that there was nothing left of the substances I'd smuggled into her apartment, either consciously or accidentally, upon my arrival—that there was nothing still slipped between books on the shelving near the door, nothing tucked under a skateboard that leaned against one wall—I finally slept, fitfully, for three straight days.

On the fourth day, I opened my eyes and asked Melissa to marry me. It wasn't quite as direct as that. I couched it in a conversation about our future, set it loose like a trial balloon, light and breezy: "We should get married!" The next day we drove to the Shamrock Social Club, a hipster tattoo parlor up the street on Sunset, across from the Roxy. An artist there inked *Shalom* inside my left biceps in Hebrew lettering, exactly like Melissa had on her arm—sort of an engagement tat.

The day after that, there was no ambiguity. We were just talking in the kitchen at some point when I suddenly and quite literally dropped down on one knee and blurted, "Will you marry me?" Melissa smiled, kissed me, then tapped the brakes slightly. "Yes, but let's just wait for the right time." I asked her to let me know when that right time would be. When we woke up the next morning, seven days after we'd met, she turned to me again and said softly, "You know what? Let's do it."

I was ecstatic. I was forty-nine, newly clean, and seeing the world again. I wanted back in.

To get married that quickly, I figured we'd have to drive to Nevada, just a few hours away. But after googling around, I learned we could do it that same day in California. I dashed out and bought a pair of plain gold wedding bands.

Meantime, I searched for a local one-stop marriage shop. True to its name, Instant Marriage LA provided in-a-moment marriage services—license, officiant, on-call minister if you chose to use their on-site Encino chapel (capacity: twenty guests). I called and asked the woman who answered if she could send someone to Melissa's apartment that evening. It was already the middle of the afternoon and the owner, a Russian immigrant named Maria Kharlash, said she was about to close but could do it the next day. I offered to pay extra and Maria drove from the Valley through rush-hour traffic.

The decision never felt rash or harebrained or reckless. It felt urgent. I felt like I'd been given a reprieve. I felt the astonishing luck of a man who'd agreed to meet a woman for coffee when it was all but impossible for him to leave a hotel room without a crack pipe in his hand, and who then fell in love at first sight—at first glance.

That initial glance was such a profound moment. I realize now that what floored me then was the reflective gaze I spotted in Melissa's eyes. She looked at me the way my brother always looked at me, the way my dad looked at me before that last, terrifying encounter in his driveway: with love, admiration, wonderment. She saw the pain and trauma inside me and still fell in love immediately. The most insidious thing about addiction, the hardest thing to overcome, is waking up unable to see the best of yourself.

Beau and Dad saw the best in me even when I wasn't at my best. Looking at them was like looking in a mirror and, instead of seeing an alcoholic or a drug addict, seeing the healthiest me reflected back. I never thought that Beau was worried I wouldn't be okay. I never thought he didn't have confidence in me. It was how we stayed connected.

When I saw Melissa that night at the Sunset Marquis, I abruptly realized how dependent I was on that reflective gaze. I remember when I did not see it in Kathleen's eyes—I carbon-date it, really, to after I was discharged from the Navy Reserve for failing that drug test in 2014. It then became so clear, a few short weeks after Beau had died, when Kathleen and I were sitting together in the therapist's office after our twenty-two-mile anniversary walk and she told me, "I'll never forgive you." That's when it hit me that I had no chance of handling the pain I was in. That's when I decided to get a drink. When you see those doubts and questions in the eyes of the person you're supposed to love the most, it breaks you in half.

In retrospect, it would've been hell to live with someone incapable of forgiving me while pretending that she had. And now, at last, I was starting to understand what Beau had been trying to tell me: it, too, had been all part of the process.

*   *   *

Around 6 p.m. on May 17, 2019, just before Maria arrived at Melissa's apartment, I called my dad to tell him I was getting married.

It took him a quick minute to take in the news; it had happened so fast, nobody in the family even knew I'd met someone. Yet he reset instantly, the way he always does. He seems incapable of not coming through when it matters most. He was thrilled that I sounded so happy.

"Honey," he said, "I knew that when you found love again, I'd get you back."

I felt the reflective gaze in his voice.

"Dad, I always had love," I replied. "And the only thing that allowed me to see it was the fact that you never gave up on me—that you always believed in me."

I passed the phone to Melissa. Dad's first words to her were the same ones that his grandmother said to the high school English teacher he'd married five years after becoming a widower.

"Thank you," my dad told Melissa, his voice soft and warm and welcoming, "for giving my boy the courage to love again."

The ceremony itself was comically surreal: sign some papers, say a few words—you're married! We did it under an awning on the apartment's airy patio. The only other person there besides Melissa, me, and Maria was the photographer from the rooftop pool who'd been part of the group who insisted I meet Melissa— and he was there by accident. He'd called right before the ceremony, unaware of what we were about to do, to say that he was walking by our place and thought he'd check in on us, see how we were. Melissa told him to come up but didn't tell him why. When he walked through the door, we enlisted him to take wedding pictures.

Wearing a sleek white jumpsuit she'd plucked out of her closet minutes earlier, Melissa looked like a million bucks. When she stepped onto the patio outside, the setting sun lit her up like a votive candle. I threw on a blue blazer, white dress shirt, and jeans; I decided not to go full Canadian tuxedo, like the day we met.

The whole thing lasted maybe ten minutes. Melissa and I exchanged extemporaneous vows about our love and commitment to each other. In a Russian accent that gave her words a kind of Old World officiousness, Maria followed with whatever an officiant is statutorily required to say by the state of California.

That was it. We were now husband and wife.

It was both bemusing and incredibly deep. Our relationship didn't feel in any way altered, except that now it was official. We had no plans to tell anybody beyond our parents, my daughters, and a few close friends. Yet the shock from the tabloid press that we knew would follow wasn't lost on us.

We simply stayed focused on each other throughout the ceremony. The purpling Hollywood Hills to the east, the downtown skyscrapers to the south, the snow-white gulls that spun up and down and around the silhouetted palm trees nearby as an orange sun dripped into the Pacific—I barely noticed any of it that evening. I simply stared into Melissa's blue eyes and felt grateful for what I saw reflected back.

Everything else—we tuned it out. There was always stuff to tune out. The noise out of Washington swirled around us even as we stood there together on that beautiful California night. After I'd talked earlier with Dad, I had to delay the service a few minutes to take another call from my lawyer. Trump had blasted me that afternoon on Fox News, demanding another investigation related to Burisma, even as Ukraine's new prosecutor general announced that same day he'd found no evidence to back Giuliani's crackpot claims.

I shook my head, hung up, and got married.

Where's Hunter?

I was right there.

I was so standing right there.

EPILOGUE

DEAR BEAU

Dear Beau,

Where are you, buddy? God, I miss you. You've never been more than a step from my thoughts since the very last time I held your hand. I promise you I'm trying my best, but I really wish you were here to give me a hug and tell me everything's going to be okay.

I never felt the ache of your absence more than the night our family stood on the stage together after Dad gave his victory speech as president-elect. He did it, Beau! He beat back a vile man with a vile mission, and he did it without lowering himself to the unprecedented depths reached by his opposition. The moment it became clear he'd won I thought of the long discussion that you, me, and Dad had during Dad's first presidential run, back when you and I were teenagers. I remember the three of us arguing passionately about whether one could become president while still being true to yourself and your principles, or whether you'd

239

be forced to employ the dark arts of negativity and cynical, self-serving politics.

We were certain then that Dad could hold onto those principles that make him who he is and still get elected to the country's highest office. It took a while—a *long* while, for sure. He had so many opportunities during this election to do to the other side what they were doing to us—to attack Trump's adult kids and family, to rile up the crazies—but he didn't.

Standing on that stage, Beau, holding your seven-month-old namesake, who Dad lifted from my arms as fireworks lit the sky, all I could think about was how proud you would've been.

You would have loved the scene on election night, too, even though the night would've driven you nuts, not least because the vote counting dragged on for days. Yet one of the benefits of waiting so long for the race to be called was that we all waited it out together, at Mom and Dad's house—Melissa and the baby, my girls, Natalie and Hunter, Ashley and Howard. More than waiting together, we were also quarantined together. There was no escaping one another.

For much of the first night, little Hunter and I sat together on the couch in the downstairs room with the big TV on, the rest of the family filtering in and out. The early returns were all over the place—we were up, we were down; we were winning Ohio, then losing Ohio. All night Hunter and I looked at each other and exchanged variations on "I hate this! Why do we put ourselves through this?" But of course we loved it. We'd yell at Natalie to sit down so we could see the TV, just like I used to get on you for hogging the remote. They're so funny and mature now, Beau.

My girls took on their own roles. Maisy made everyone laugh with her wry observations. Finnegan was full of insight. She'd sit by Mom and Dad and give specific edits as Dad reviewed speeches he gave to update supporters and the rest of the country as that night and the following days wore on. Even with Ron Klain, Mike Donilon, and Aunt Val giving their own advice over speaker phone, Finnegan had the confidence to voice what she thought. And then there was Naomi—God, you'd love Naomi. She has this sense of poise and elegance and grace—and the driest wit. They miss you so much, Beau.

The night played out exactly how you would've hoped. It was the culmination of what you once told Dad: no matter what happened, he couldn't give up. I know you didn't mean he necessarily had to keep running for president, but that he did have to continue to have the purpose that holds this family together.

Throughout the campaign Trump attacked everyone in the family in the harshest, most horrible terms. But instead of tearing us apart, the barrage of assaults accomplished the opposite: they allowed us to fully heal again. That first night, when the networks called Florida and Ohio for Trump, and we trailed in Michigan, Pennsylvania, and Wisconsin, the family didn't devolve into a circular firing squad. Everybody just curled up on the couch together. Win, lose, or draw, nothing was going to change that.

Given the place I was in only a year and a half earlier, I felt blessed. A little before midnight, before Dad left to give an update in front of a crowd honking car horns at a drive-in rally, I told him what we always told him: no matter what, we'd already won. I felt for him, though. It was a Herculean task to project confidence at a moment when people around the world were trying to figure out how this election could even be close.

By the time I went to bed, at 3 a.m., the sense of dread everyone felt was overwhelming. Melissa had already fallen asleep and I spent the rest of the night staring up at the ceiling. I tried not to think dark thoughts, but it was hard not to think that what Melissa and I had feared most might come to pass. Those early hours, before the vast majority of our outstanding votes had been counted, felt perilous. A Trump victory was not only a threat to democracy, it also seemed a threat to my personal freedom. If Dad hadn't won, I'm certain Trump would've continued to pursue me in the criminal fashion he'd adopted from the start.

Then I woke up the next morning, and the morning after that, and everybody was still together and the election had begun to turn. One of Melissa's many gifts to me is the understanding that everything happens in its own time, if you allow it to. As long as I'm sober and healthy and available, good things will come.

Four days after the election, on a glorious Saturday morning, I was sitting in the sunroom with all the girls, Natalie and Hunter, Melissa and baby Beau, Ashley and Howard, and Annie and Anthony—when the networks called Pennsylvania for Dad. That clinched it. Mom and Dad were on a dock out on the pond, so we all ran to the porch and screamed at the top of our lungs, "We won! We just won!"

It was a moment of relief, exhaustion, and absolute joy. By the time the counting finished, more Americans had voted for Dad than for any president in history. Still more amazing is the level of decency and integrity he brings to the office—exactly what the three of us ultimately determined was possible those many years ago. Neither Dad nor I said that aloud. We didn't have to. We hugged and kissed instead.

I've survived, buddy. I know you were with me through it all. They came after me with everything they had. It was all "Where's Hunter?" all the time. But it turned out they did me an unintended favor. I became the beneficiary of the absurdity and transparent criminality of my pursuers. Each attack added to my new superpower: the ability to absorb their negative energy and use it to make me stronger. It was like political aikido. Every bogus whistleblower, out-of-context email, salacious photograph or video clip (manufactured or real), made me feel nearly invincible to their slings and arrows.

They doubled down on the notion I wouldn't be strong enough to maintain my sobriety, that I'd crack and they'd pounce. But here's what they didn't count on, Beau: you were with me the whole way, in the form of Melissa and baby Beau, my girls, our sister, our aunts and uncles, Mom and Dad. Everyone. Your strength and love was embodied in the strength and love that surrounded me.

That was never truer than when Giuliani, Bannon, and their collaborators purported to have a laptop that chronicled the lurid details of my descent into addiction the last three years. What should have been the most anxiety-producing event of an anxiety-producing campaign became a televised burlesque. I turned to

Melissa at one point and said, "You'd think this would make me want to drink. But it's the furthest thing from my mind."

In that moment, I knew there was absolutely nothing they could do to take away this beautiful thing I'd built. When they finished, Melissa and I simply went about our day. We made lunch. We took baby Beau to the beach to watch the sunset.

Here's my takeaway: the ability to shrug everything off and carry on, two weeks before the most consequential election in our lifetimes, was the result of the thousands of expressions of love given to me and that I'd given back. Talking to my girls every day; knowing Melissa was always there for me in the next room; looking up from my desk to see baby Beau's big, toothless smile aimed directly at me—I'm living in those moments and not in the shitstorm I couldn't control.

I took solace in being attacked by such despicable opposition. When you're assaulted by people with the capacity to take away an infant suckling from his mother's breast and place him in a cage—well, I knew I was playing on the right side. I knew that if I could hold on and have the strength to ride out the attacks, justice would be done. It doesn't always happen that way. But it happened that way this time.

Dad, of course, never flinched. A turning point in the campaign was the first debate, and a turning point in that debate came when Dad talked about you. Trump played the only card he ever plays: attack. In that moment, the difference between the two men was never starker.

We knew he'd attack me. Before the debate, I told Dad not to duck when Trump brought me up, as I was sure he would. I told him that I wasn't embarrassed about what I'd faced to overcome my addiction. I told him that there were tens of millions of families who would relate to it, whether because of their own struggles or the struggles being faced by someone they loved. Not only was I comfortable with him talking about it, I believed it needed to be said.

He said it. While Dad was honoring your service in Iraq as a response to the leaks that Trump had called Americans who fought in wars "losers" and "suckers," Trump interrupted with his trademark callousness and went after me.

Dad countered artfully, empathetically, indelibly.

"My son," he said, ignoring Trump while looking straight into a camera, "like a lot of people you know at home, had a drug problem. He's overtaken it, he's fixed it, he's worked on it. And I'm proud of him. I'm proud of my son."

Those words not only disarmed Trump but gave comfort and hope to millions of Americans. I felt nothing but pride. You would've, too.

Beau, I'm finally living a life you always wanted me to. You'd love California, you'd love where I live. There are so many beautiful things to be grateful for, and I try to remind myself to look at them every day. We've been in a lockdown because of the pandemic but I'm not really missing the outside world all that much. I have Melissa and baby Beau and my girls. I have the whole family. I've been writing. I've returned to painting.

I've been painting like crazy. It's kept me grounded, and initially kept me away from that underworld just down the canyon from us. It unlocked something that had been trying to emerge from inside me since, well, since we were kids. I finally have the time and space—and sobriety—to explore it.

Now, I wake up with baby Beau, make a cup of coffee, and paint through the morning. Then Melissa makes us lunch. Sometimes we take a walk, sometimes we take a drive. Then I paint through the afternoon, my hands and forearms covered in blues and yellows and greens. I'm driven to create.

For all the art I've made since I was a kid—art that only you ever really saw—and the sketchbooks I've filled over the years, I feel like I've returned to my authentic self. Whether anybody likes it or not isn't what drives to me to get up to paint. I paint no matter what. I paint because I want to. I paint because I have to. Our house is filled with paintings.

It's all part of a new chapter, another step in the process. I still have a ton of work to do on myself, with my addiction, and clearing the wreckage of my past. I'm trying to make good on my debts—both figurative and literal.

I don't want to give the impression I think my problems are over and everything's great. You know as well as anyone how I've experienced long-term sobriety only to have it vanish in an instant. I'm constantly aware that it can be fleeting and fragile. I'm constantly aware of how much danger I'm in no matter how far away I get from my last drink or drug. But I'm not hanging on by my fingernails this time; the desire, the itch, to use is gone.

I learned this during my first rehab stint, back in 2003: Sobriety is easy, all you have to do is change everything. Part of that change for me is no longer allowing myself the selfish pleasure of reacting in the same old ways to the same old things. I know now I don't have the luxury of staying angry. I don't have the luxury of wallowing in self-pity or frustration. I don't have the luxury of being offended by people because of their concerns for me, whether legitimate or stemming from their own issues.

I don't have the luxury of saying *fuck it*.

I talk every day with folks who are in recovery. With addiction as the equalizer, I've developed a support network of people who understand the struggle based on their own struggles. We rarely talk about those struggles in any specific way. Mostly we just talk: about what we're grateful for, about something in the news that really gripes us. We're making sure our connections are active in our daily lives so that they're fully available in a moment of crisis. You never know when that moment will come. Even when the ghosts of addiction have been banished, they still exist. I have a healthy fear of them.

I'm focused on our children. The time I lost with them remains my greatest regret. We're getting there. There's a sense that all the horrible things said about me have brought us closer together, made them more fiercely loyal. That gives us an opportunity for healing. I love what Hemingway wrote: "The world breaks everyone and afterward many are strong in the broken places." That's my hope. All wounds don't heal overnight.

What I've been through—what I've done—is something I can never purge, never forget. But I'm learning to live in the moment without constantly feeling guilt or shame. Credit for that goes to Melissa. To Naomi, Finnegan, and Maisy. To our family. To you.

I don't fear the future anymore, Beau. I realized it a few weeks before the election. In the middle of all the salacious attacks on me, a friend wondered aloud, "Wouldn't it be great if this whole story had a happy ending?"

And I thought, this story already has a happy ending. The happy ending began the day I met Melissa and finally put down the drink and drugs. Despite all of the pressure and having to deal with the consequences of my irresponsibilities, the happy ending is right here. But a happy ending isn't the end, or a finish line—it's just the beginning, the beginning of a life I have to work to keep every day, a life I am lucky to live as long as I stay sober.

And what an incredible gift it is: to live in the light of beautiful things.

God, I miss you, buddy.

I love you. I love you. I love you.

Hunter

AFTERWORD

The moment we're living through as a country, and the place I occupy in that moment as a recovering alcoholic and addict, came at me full-force on a beautiful fall afternoon seven months after this book was first published.

It was Halloween, 2021. My family and I had just finished lunch at an outdoor restaurant near our home in California. I was with Melissa, my toddler son, Beau, and my father-in-law, Lee, who was visiting us for the first time from his home in South Africa. Lee had recently lost his wife of fifty-four years—Melissa's mother, Zoe—to cancer. Because of the pandemic, he was seeing his grandson in person for the first time.

With Beau perched atop my shoulders, already dressed for Halloween in a Chewbacca outfit, we headed for our car. That's when I noticed a man and a woman, both of whom looked to be in their early sixties, running in our direction.

The man held out a phone, clearly recording whatever was about to happen. The woman, meanwhile, rushed at us in a rage, both of her middle fingers extended and aimed directly at me, all while she screamed obscenities.

We ducked into the car before they reached us. Melissa was shaken, holding Beau tight to her chest in the back seat. Lee sat wide-eyed beside me. Neither could believe anyone would spew that kind of venom at somebody carrying a nineteen-month-old on his shoulders.

I assured Melissa that everything was fine, then calmed everyone as we made our way back home.

As someone who's been involved in politics his entire life, the scene captured everything about where much of the country is right now: gripped by an irrational anger I've never witnessed before.

The world saw that anger erupt ten months earlier, on January 6, 2021, when insurrectionists stormed the U.S. Capitol. But my family and I have faced variations of it up close, over and over—whether it's the red-capped herd camped outside our house shouting through a bullhorn that forced us to move; the social media posts that conjure up the most deranged stories about me; or the elderly couple who turned our son's first Halloween into a real-life nightmare.

The state of my recovery was also on display that afternoon in Malibu. Not for the man with the camera, but for myself and my family and anyone else who cares for me. I didn't react the way the couple who'd been spoon-fed so many lies by Rudy Giuliani and Steve Bannon and Donald Trump's other capos hoped I'd react.

When I got home, I didn't do what I did throughout much of what is described in this book: reach for a drink or a drug. Or both.

My inaction—my choice to detach from outcomes I have no control over—is the best answer to the question many readers asked when they finished reading the first edition of this book:

Can he stay clean and sober?

I'm still clean and sober today.

I expect to be clean and sober tomorrow.

My family and friends reacted to the book with relief—that I was alive.

They were shocked at the depth of my addiction. Some let me know how hurt they were by my actions, how bewildered and troubled my disappearances left them. Others called to apologize for not knowing how bad things had gotten, believing they could have done something for me if only they'd known more.

Nobody needed to apologize, of course. They were never going to know more. I was too good at being an addict. Lots of us are.

Reading this memoir was hardest for my daughters. They lived through the pain it describes, but from a distance. To have a front-row seat now, through these pages, was gut-wrenching. It forced them to relive a period that impacted them most profoundly by my absence.

This book told them where I was. Among the many, many, many sins I committed during that time, not being there for my daughters is the greatest sin of all.

I'm sure their feelings are mixed, confused, in flux. But that's not for me to say. A lot of healing remains to be done.

Despite my family's and friends' relief, their optimism remains cautious. They've been around recovery enough to know how tenuous it is. I've let them down before. Their skepticism is hard-earned.

The dirty little secret: success is rare. I'm Exhibit A. People see the enormous pressure of the public shaming directed at me every day and can't help but be concerned.

The concern is genuine. It's also frustrating. Yet I'm past reassuring everybody and instead I remind them that the proof is in the pudding: the only way addicts can allay the fears of those most concerned about them is to stay clean. That's what I have to do daily. Not tell people that I'm clean, just show them.

The ghosts feel less threatening.

Since getting clean, I've avoided the people and places from the darkest parts of my past. Melissa has helped me keep all of that at bay.

While writing the book, however, a friend suggested taking a kind of drive-by tour of some of my old L.A. haunts. Not as a dare or an exorcism, but merely as a way to trigger some details lost to those too-high times. Places like the Chateau Marmont, where my madness swelled to new heights; the club on Hollywood Boulevard where Baby Down pulled me from a pair of enraged bouncers and cooled me off as we sat among all the other late-night denizens inside Mel's Diner, on the Strip; the downtown tent city, where my madness hit new depths as I stared down the barrel of a gun.

The trip sounded like a good idea. We'd make the rounds in the morning, the most harmless time of that landscape's day. My friend would ride along.

Then, as we were about to leave the house I'd rented at the time in the Hollywood Hills, high above all that, Melissa called from an early food run she'd made to let me know she was on her way back. I told her what I was about to do, that I might not be there when she arrived, but that I wouldn't be gone long. I'd never heard panic like that in her voice. She implored me not go and wouldn't hang up until I promised. She still feared the power of those ghosts.

I stayed home.

Two years later, in November 2021, we flew to New York for a reception at a Soho gallery exhibiting my art. I stopped by the night before the reception to see how the show looked. Finnegan, Maisie, and Melissa's dad came with me.

Afterward, we walked back to the hotel. It was a perfect fall evening. A few blocks into our trip, I suddenly realized we were in a part of Soho where I'd spent too many nights being up to no good. I recognized restaurants and lounges and speakeasies; I passed one in particular where I'd gotten loaded plenty of times. I noted how it no longer had its old power over me.

"Wow," I said aloud to myself, "I just passed Lucky Strike."

I didn't fear it. I didn't long for it. I didn't even notice that it had been closed. The only thought I had as I passed it was how much I wanted to get back to the hotel and cuddle with baby Beau.

I'd had a full day. I was beat. I wanted to go to bed. And even that was a revelation. Three years earlier, if I was that tired, the last thing I'd do is go to sleep. I'd get anxious about whatever I had to do the next day, and then, because I didn't want to feel anxious, I'd drop into one of the Soho bars I was passing and blast away the feeling with drinks or drugs—anything to take me out of myself.

Now I felt tired, ready to close down, eager to get up early the next day. I just wanted to get to where I was supposed to go, taking one step after the other.

I don't go to AA meetings in the traditional sense now. I think— no, I know—it's helpful, and it has helped me in the past. But it's impossible for me to go to meetings now in any constructive way. I can't maintain anonymity, and I can't talk on Zoom without fear of someone taping me.

But every day I talk with someone in the program, someone working their recovery. I've surrounded myself with people in my daily life who've gone through the same experiences, people who are making the choice to practice the things that keep them clean.

That's what recovery is: the realization you have a choice every day. I don't have to pick up a drink or a drug today. If I don't, my options are limitless.

I'm proof you can't give up. I'm fully aware I'm blessed in ways few others are, that I've had advantages because of the family I was born into. Yet this stuff still isn't easy. I'm still someone who was locked in a prison of putting a glass pipe to my lips for two years straight and who lost everything that mattered. I know what it's like to not be free from the wreckage of my past and have to deal with it.

Interviewing me about my book for New York's 92nd Street Y, writer Anne Lamott underscored that fact in a way that floored me. Annie, too, is a recovering alcoholic and drug addict. So is her son.

"Even though we have literally nothing in common biographically," she said to me by way of introduction, "we share the one biggest, truest detail of all: we are born to die addicts and alcoholics in recovery."

That's all of us.

I get up each morning at 5:30. The joints in my knees no longer feel like they're frozen together; I don't feel the need to run to the bathroom and puke. While the spectacular realization of what it's like to be sober fades a few months after getting clean, the pride you have in yourself, and the sense of overwhelming serenity, remains. Both those things are part of what I say to myself when I wake up and go through my gratitude list. I do it every day.

Then I get Beau out of his crib, carry him to the kitchen and put him in his high chair. I give him bananas and berries for breakfast and make coffee and tea for me and Melissa.

When we finish, Beau and I head to the backyard to see if we can spot one of the wild parrots that flit around in our trees. We then walk over to my studio, turn on the lights, and open the doors and windows to let even more light inside. Beau helps me set up for the day.

Then I paint.

I am exactly where I'm supposed to be, doing exactly what I'm supposed to be doing. That became clear the night my paintings were shown publicly for the first time, at a gallery in Los Angeles, before a gathering of almost two hundred people.

As we were all getting ready at the house, my daughter Naomi asked me if I was nervous. I told her no, not at all. About an hour later, as we got closer to leaving, she asked me again. No, I said, still not nervous. When I gave her the same answer to the same question as we all were about to walk out the door, Naomi looked exasperated.

"Dad," she said, "you not being nervous is making me *really* nervous."

I laughed.

"Honey," I told her, "all the work is done. I'm incredibly proud of it and that's all that matters. I get to walk into an exhibit and see it all framed and lit in a way that makes it more special. And I get to share it with you guys, with my daughters. What could I possibly be nervous about?"

I don't think I could've chosen anything further away from the business of politics than art, yet that same cast of bad actors have tried to take even that away.

I won't let them. I have to admit to a perverse kind of joy in knowing the way I feel about my life right now is completely contrary to the way Rudy and Don and Eric think they're making me feel. I've had a show at a New York gallery and I've had legitimate critics assess my work—the good, the bad, and the meh. I'll take it.

I've never been happier in my own skin. I've never felt more content. I'll never take it for granted.

The public discourse provoked by the book revealed what I knew in my heart to be true: there is no one who has not been touched by addiction.

Not a single reporter or host who interviewed me during my book tour—nor a single stranger I met and talked with about the book—failed to share a story of addiction's effects in their lives, whether with a family member, a co-worker, a friend, or themselves.

One interviewer did tell me that he didn't understand how I experienced the things I wrote about. The lows were just too low, he said. It pissed him off. He got angry at the main character—i.e., me—because of what I was doing. He said he'd never known anyone who'd fallen that far, gotten that depraved.

So before interviewing me, he called his oldest friend, a recovering alcoholic and addict, and asked him to read the book. He wanted to know if his friend could identify with it, especially the darkest passages.

"Yeah," his friend told him after reading it. "Everything."

The interviewer was shocked at how far I had fallen, yet his oldest friend had once been right down there with me, so to speak, as have so many other addicts and alcoholics.

The coda to the story: it opened an honest conversation between two people who'd been friends for almost fifty years about something that is often still taboo to talk about. Because of that conversation, the interviewer came to understand, and have a new empathy for, someone he clearly loved.

With stories like that, my hope for this book was being realized. If the son of a U.S. president can engage in an honest conversation about addiction in front of the world, then maybe two lifelong friends—or a mother and son, or a brother and sister, or a husband and wife—can find the courage to have an honest conversation about addiction in the privacy of their own homes.

We're getting there.

ACKNOWLEDGMENTS

Thank you to Drew Jubera, without whom *Beautiful Things* would not have been possible, and to the outstanding team behind this book: Andrew Chaikivsky, Laura Nolan and David Granger at Aevitas, Jack Kingsrud, Kevin Morris, and George Mesires.

Thank you to Aimée Bell and everyone at Gallery Books: Jennifer Bergstrom, Jennifer Long, Sally Marvin, Max Meltzer, Eric Rayman, Jennifer Robinson, Tom Spain, Jennifer Weidman, Sarah Wright, and Laura Cherkas.

Thank you to my family, and to everyone who helped me on this path toward beautiful things.

Thank you especially to Naomi, Finnegan, and Maisy.

Most of all: Thank you, Melissa, the love of my life.

Hunt –
The Bravest Boy + Man
I've ever known –
I love you more
than the whole
sky
Dad
12-25-18